PRAISE FOR *BIG LONELY DOUG*

FINALIST, SHAUGHNESSY COHEN PRIZE FOR POLITICAL WRITING
FINALIST, RODERICK HAIG-BROWN REGIONAL PRIZE
FINALIST, BANFF MOUNTAIN BOOK COMPETITION
A *GLOBE AND MAIL* TOP 100 BOOK

"[Rustad's] microscale descriptions of the landscape and how commercial forestry has changed it bring you into the depths of Vancouver Island."
— *Outside Magazine*

"[A] very timely narrative." — *Toronto Star*

"[Harley Rustad] is a gifted researcher and writer and a valuable enabler whose book is a must-read for anyone interested in ecology."
— *Winnipeg Free Press*

"Rustad, a Salt Spring Island native, digs into the B.C. psyche with his discussions of old growth forests, big trees, the logging industry, ecotourism, and First Nations rights and issues." — *Vancouver Sun*

"May change the way you interact with forests or, at the very least, individual trees." — *Globe and Mail*

"[An] absorbing story of how the human fixation on individuals turned one tree into an icon of both ecotourism and resource extraction."
— *Maclean's*

"In the face of global ecological chaos, how much does one tree matter? For Harley Rustad, one in particular — a twenty-storey Douglas fir standing on Vancouver Island — matters enough to make it the star of a brilliant story about the challenges, losses, and triumphs of conservation today. Rustad is a careful reporter and an excellent storyteller, combining these skills to weave together the ecology of British Columbia and the politics of contemporary environmentalism into a single engaging narrative about Big Lonely Doug, one of Canada's last great trees."
— Shaughnessy Cohen Prize
for Political Writing Jury Citation

"Among the joys of good writing and deep research are the ways in which it can reinvigorate a place you thought you knew, inviting you to see it, and feel it, afresh. This is just one of the gifts of Big Lonely Doug, an avatar of the west coast rainforest that, through Harley Rustad's insightful and nuanced telling, embodies this vital ecosystem in all its beauty and complexity. Reading this book made me want to drop everything and meet Doug in person."

— John Vaillant, author of *The Golden Spruce*

"Having spent time, personally, with Big Lonely Doug, and wandering through the last of our ancient forests in British Columbia, it's never been more clear to me how imperative it is for us as humans to recognize the magnificence of these ancient trees and forests and do everything that we can to preserve them. With less than 1 percent of the original old-growth Douglas fir stands left on B.C.'s coast, it's time for Canadians to embrace Big Lonely Doug and his fellow survivors, and keep them standing tall. Harley Rustad's story brings both the majesty and adversity of Big Lonely Doug a little closer to home." — Edward Burtynsky

"You *can* see the forest for the trees, at least when the trees in question are singular giants like Big Lonely Doug, and the writer deftly directing your gaze is Harley Rustad. This sweeping yet meticulous narrative reveals the complex human longings tangled up in B.C.'s vanishing old-growth forests — cathedrals or commodities, depending on who you ask, and the future hinges on our answer."

— Kate Harris, author of *Lands of Lost Borders*

"An affecting story of one magnificent survivor tree set against a much larger narrative — the old conflict between logging and the environmental movement, global economics, and the fight to preserve the planet's most endangered ecosystems. If you love trees and forests, this book is for you."

— Charlotte Gill, author of *Eating Dirt*

"Blending thoughtful historical research with vivid reportage, Harley Rustad begins with the story of a single tree but masterfully widens his scope to encompass so much more: all the other grand old trees that have been felled on Vancouver Island, all those that have been saved, and most importantly, why it all matters. A complex and at times alarming tale, but also, in the end, a deeply hopeful one."

— Robert Moor, author of *On Trails*

The Walrus Books

The Walrus sparks essential Canadian conversation by publishing high-quality, fact-based journalism and producing ideas-focused events across the country. The Walrus Books, a partnership between *The Walrus*, House of Anansi Press, and the Chawkers Foundation Writers Project, supports the creation of Canadian non-fiction books of national interest.

Big Lonely Doug is the first in this series.
thewalrus.ca/books

BIG LONELY DOUG

The Story of One of Canada's Last Great Trees

Harley Rustad

ANANSI

Published in Canada in 2018 and the USA in 2019 by
House of Anansi Press Inc.

www.houseofanansi.com

House of Anansi Press is committed to protecting our natural environment. This book is made of material from well-managed FSC®-certified forests, recycled materials, and other controlled sources.

House of Anansi Press is a Global Certified Accessible™ (GCA by Benetech) publisher. The ebook version of this book meets stringent accessibility standards and is available to readers with print disabilities.

28 27 26 25 24 6 7 8 9 10

Library and Archives Canada Cataloguing in Publication

Rustad, Harley, author
Big Lonely Doug / Harley Rustad.
Issued in print and electronic formats.
ISBN 978-1-4870-0311-1 (softcover). — ISBN 978-1-4870-0312-8 (EPUB). —
ISBN 978-1-4870-0313-5 (Kindle)
1. Old growth forest ecology—British Columbia. 2. Old growth forest conservation—British Columbia. 3. Logging—British Columbia. 4. Ecotourism—British Columbia. I. Title.

QH106.2.B7R87 2018 577.309711 C2018-900673-0
C2018-900674-9

Library of Congress Control Number: 2018943835

Book design: Alysia Shewchuk
Map of Vancouver Island: Mary Rostad

House of Anansi Press is grateful for the privilege to work on and create from the Traditional Territory of many Nations, including the Anishinabeg, the Wendat, and the Haudenosaunee, as well as the Treaty Lands of the Mississaugas of the Credit.

With the participation of the Government of Canada
Avec la participation du gouvernement du Canada | Canada

We acknowledge for their financial support of our publishing program the Canada Council for the Arts, the Ontario Arts Council, and the Government of Canada.

Printed and bound in Canada

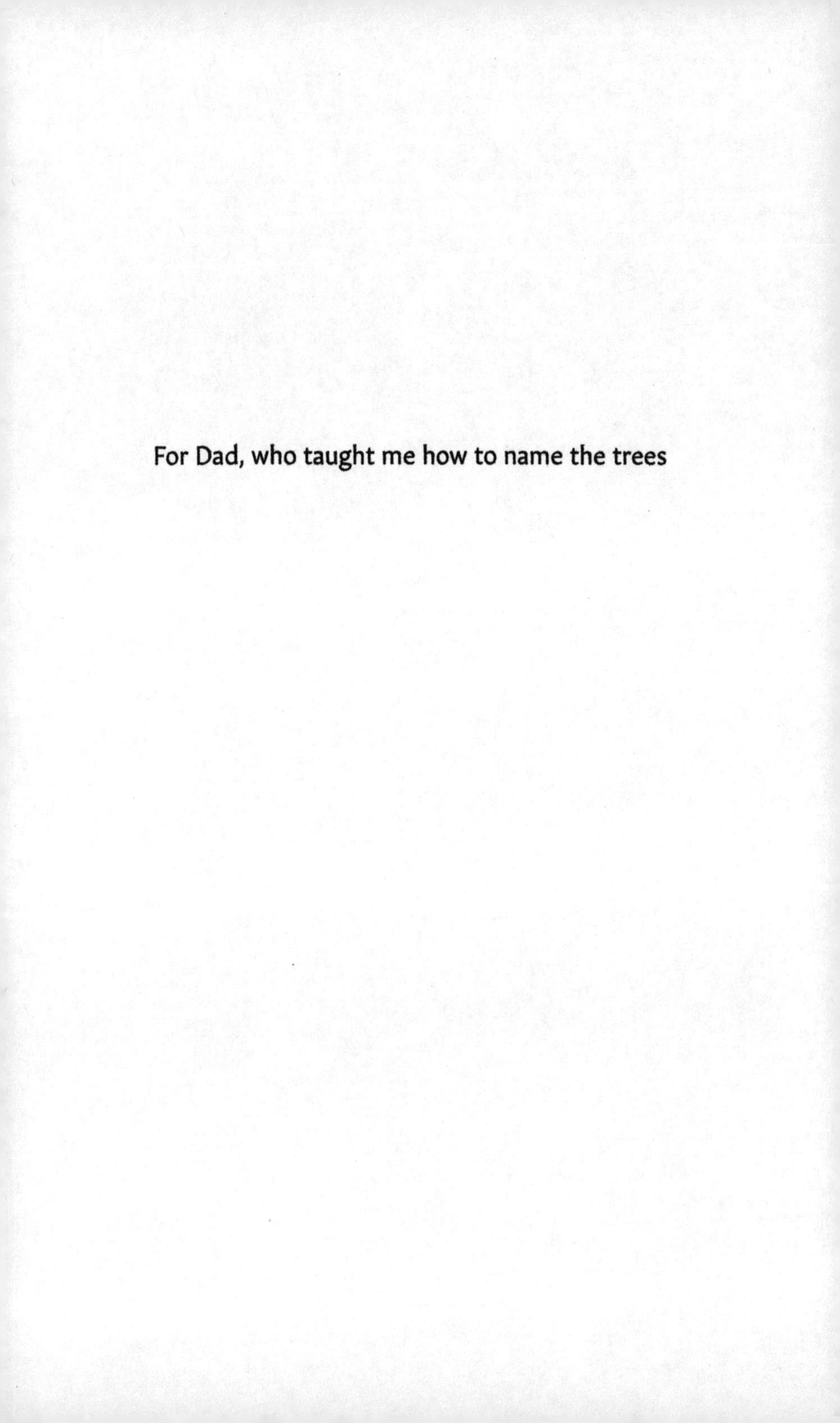

For Dad, who taught me how to name the trees

CONTENTS

Prologue: A Seed 1

Chapter 1: The Ribbon 5
Chapter 2: Evergreen. 13
Chapter 3: A Tree of Many Names 31
Chapter 4: Green Gold 51
Chapter 5: War for the Woods 85
Chapter 6: A Forest Alliance. 115
Chapter 7: The Logger 153
Chapter 8: Last Tree Standing 165
Chapter 9: Growing an Icon 177
Chapter 10: Big Tree Hunting. 193
Chapter 11: Tall Tree Capital. 213
Chapter 12: A New Ecosystem 233
Epilogue: A Giant 257

Notes *277*
Acknowledgements. *301*
Index *305*

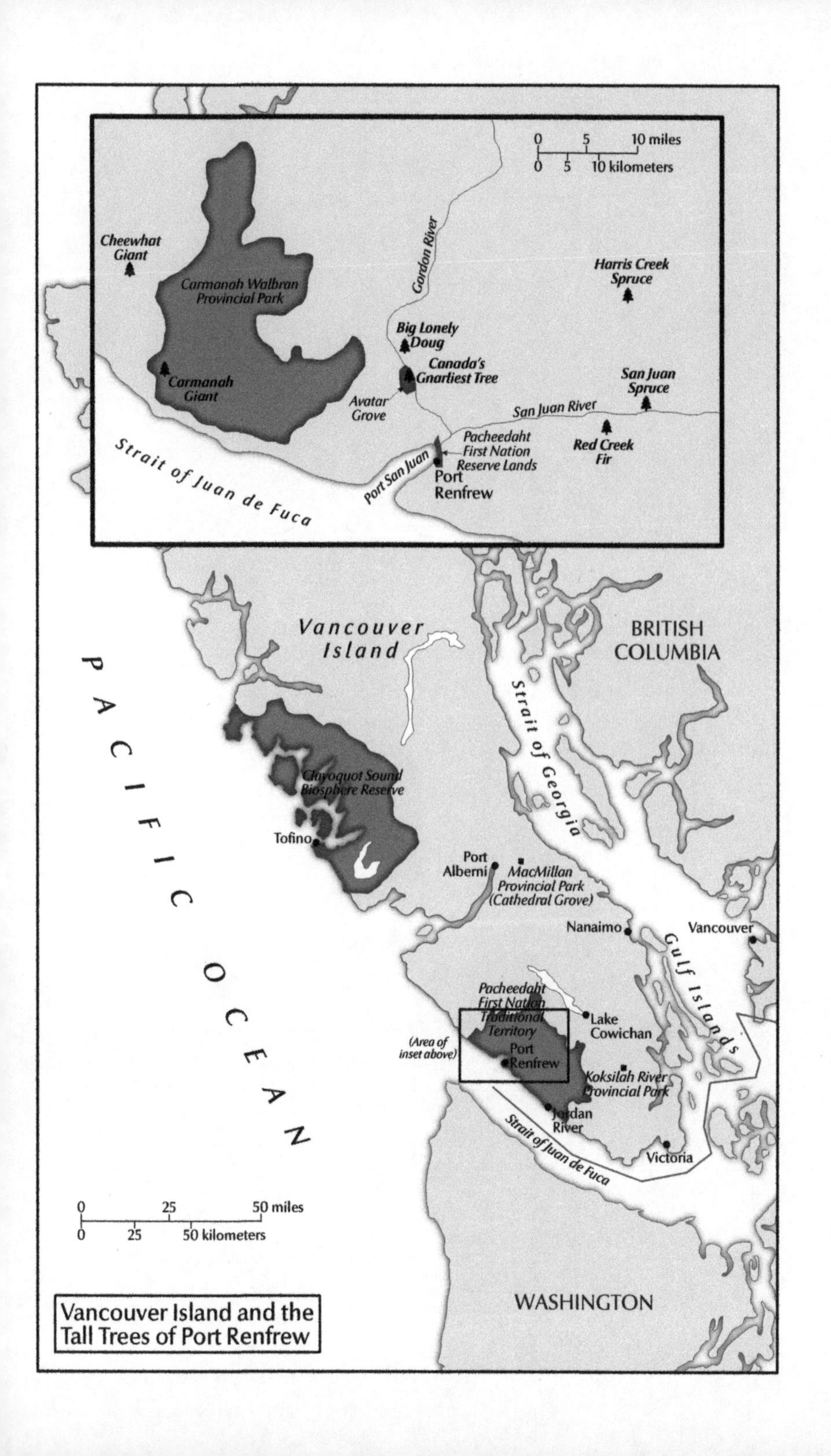

0 5 10 miles
0 5 10 kilometers
Cheewhat Giant
Carmanah Walbran Provincial Park
Gordon River
Harris Creek Spruce
Big Lonely Doug
Canada's Gnarliest Tree
Carmanah Giant
Avatar Grove
San Juan Spruce
San Juan River
Pacheedaht First Nation Reserve Lands
Red Creek Fir
Port San Juan
Port Renfrew
Strait of Juan de Fuca
Vancouver Island
BRITISH COLUMBIA
PACIFIC OCEAN
Strait of Georgia
Clayoquot Sound Biosphere Reserve
Tofino
Port Alberni
MacMillan Provincial Park (Cathedral Grove)
Nanaimo
Vancouver
Gulf Islands
Pacheedaht First Nation Traditional Territory
Lake Cowichan
(Area of inset above)
Port Renfrew
Koksilah River Provincial Park
Jordan River
Strait of Juan de Fuca
Victoria
0 25 50 miles
0 25 50 kilometers
WASHINGTON
Vancouver Island and the Tall Trees of Port Renfrew

PROLOGUE

A Seed

A CALM WIND RUFFLED THE branches of some of the largest trees in the world. It twisted and turned through the forest, picking up scents of cedar and fir and spruce — even a faint tinge of salt, this close to the Pacific Ocean. Late afternoon sun had burned off any lingering mist, leaving a clear blue sky.

Nearly every branch on nearly every tree held cones that dangled like ornaments. On one tree, a Douglas fir growing in a valley on Vancouver Island, a cone shook and bounced in the breeze. It began to open. The warm season had caused the cone's colour to gradually turn from green and sticky with sap to brown and papery dry, its thumbnail-shaped scales to separate, and the species' telltale trident-like bracts to curl — the final stage in the cone's year-and-a-half cycle to maturation.

As the temperature fluctuated between the early autumn's hot days and cool nights, the cone responded accordingly, opening and closing so slightly it would be nearly imperceptible to the eye. One degree of seasonal difference could spell disaster for the precious seeds held within the cone: too hot and they might dry out; too cold and wet and they might rot.

As the sun began to drop behind the forested hills, and when the moisture in the air was just right, a seed dislodged from between the scales and began tumbling earthwards alongside the great trunk of its parent tree. Its feathery tail twirled slightly in the freefall towards a dense undergrowth of salal, sword fern, and huckleberry—a fall where the randomness of nature would determine its fate.

The vast majority of the fifty thousand seeds that fell from each tree that year would die. They would be eaten by birds or squirrels or would simply not be lucky enough to find the optimal conditions to sprout. But this one survived. This one landed softly on a patch of moist, green moss growing on the rotting bark of a tree that had been blown over by a fierce wind a century before. Feeding off nutrients in the log, the seed pushed through the moss and into the light. The seedling, barely an inch tall, spread its first pair of glossy green needles.

In time, the seedling would enter an exalted arboreal pantheon, which included some of Canada's biggest trees: western red cedars so wide that it would take ten people holding hands in a chain to encircle their bases; Sitka spruces so tall that their tops would rival towers of a city core; and Douglas firs so old they would outlive more than a dozen human generations. In the wet valleys would grow the epitomes of their respective species—great, hulking masses of nature.

These trees would come to attract the attention of loggers, who would put axe and saw to trunk to harvest the warm wood that could be cut and manipulated for innumerable uses. These trees would be surrounded by protestors fighting for their protection, seeing more value in keeping them alive than in their immediate utility. And these trees would attract visitors who wanted little more than to feel awe and wonder in the shadow of one of nature's giants.

The seedling grew into a sapling—and then it grew into a tree.

CHAPTER 1

The Ribbon

ON A COOL MORNING in the winter of 2011, Dennis Cronin parked his truck by the side of a dirt logging road, laced up his spike-soled caulk boots, put on his red cargo vest and orange hard hat, and stepped into the trees. He had a job to do: walk a stand of old-growth forest and flag it for clear-cutting.

In many ways, this patch of forest was unremarkable. Cronin had spent four decades traipsing through tens of thousands of similar hectares of lush British Columbia rainforest, and had stood under hundreds of giant, ancient trees. Over his career in the logging industry, he had seen the seemingly inexhaustible resource of big timber continue to dwindle, and the unbroken evergreen that once covered Vancouver Island reduced to rare and isolated groves.

Known as cutblock number 7190 by his employer, one of the largest timber companies operating on the island, the twelve hectares represented a small sliver—around the size of twelve football fields—of the kind of old-growth forest that once spanned the island nearly from tip to tip and coast to coast. But this small patch of trees fringing the left bank of the Gordon River, just north of the small seaside town of Port Renfrew, was a prime example of an endangered ecosystem. Black bears and elk, wolves and cougars passed quietly under its canopy. Red-capped woodpeckers knocked on standing deadwood; squirrels and chipmunks nibbled on cones to extract seeds; and fungi the size of dinner plates protruded from the trunks of some of the largest trees in the world.

Cronin brushed through the salal and fern undergrowth, his jeans wet with dew that even during a hot summer forms every morning in these forests of perpetual damp. Underfoot, mounds of moss covering a thick bed of decaying tree needles were soft and spongy. Sounds don't linger in these forests, arriving and dissipating quickly—absorbed by thicket and peat and mist before they're allowed to swell. For now, the forest was still.

Cronin began the survey along the low edge of cutblock 7190, where he could hear the Gordon River thundering on the other side of a steep gorge. Come spring, salmon fry would be wriggling free of the pebbled river bottom and making their first swim downstream to open water; come fall, mature fish would hurl themselves upstream to spawn. The ancient trees, with their dense tangle of roots growing along the banks of the river, would filter out sediment and loose soil so that even during a rainstorm the forest kept the waters running clear.

As a forest engineer, Cronin's job involved walking the contours of the cutblock, taking stock of the timber, and producing a map for the fallers to follow. At regular intervals of a couple dozen metres or so, he reached into his vest pocket for a roll of neon orange plastic ribbon and tore off a strip. The colour had to be bright to catch the eye of the fallers who would follow in the weeks or months to come. He tied the inch-wide sashes around small trees or the low-hanging branches of hemlocks or cedars to mark the edges of the cutblock. "FALLING BOUNDARY" was repeated along each ribbon. Timber companies in the province follow a forestry code stipulating that forest engineers must leave an intact buffer of fifty metres of forest up from a river, especially one that is known to be a spawning ground for salmon. Some engineers keep tight to those regulations to try to extract as much timber as possible from a given area. Known as "timber pigs," they work the bush under a singular mantra: log it, burn it, pave it. The sentiment is twofold: ecology is secondary to economics, and these forests exist to be harvested. But Cronin was often generous with these buffer zones, leaving sixty to seventy-five metres—as much as he could without drawing the ire of co-workers or bosses.

There were trees of every age: a handful of exceptionally large cedars and firs, many younger and thinner hemlocks, and saplings filling in the gaps. The sun broke through the canopy in long beams that spotlit sword ferns and huckleberry bushes on the forest floor. Patches of lime-green moss turned highlighter-fluorescent in the sun. Scattered clouds broke an unusually clear blue sky; Cronin was more used to working amid thick mist and showers on winter days, emerging from a forest soaked and chilled.

Once the boundary of the twelve hectares was flagged with orange ribbon, Cronin criss-crossed the cutblock, surveying the pitches and gradients of the land. It was a slow task, clambering over slippery fallen logs and through thickets of bush. At one point, he climbed up onto a log to determine where a road could be ploughed into the forest. In many cutblocks, the first step in harvesting the timber is to construct a road—a channel through the bush where logs can be hauled, loaded onto trucks, and transported to a mill. It takes a specific skill to see through dense forest and haphazard undergrowth and plot a sure course that will allow for the safest and easiest extraction of logs. Maneuvering over undulating land layered with deadfall and vegetation, Cronin marked a direct line through the forest with strips off another roll of ribbon, this one hot pink and marked with the words "ROAD LOCATION." He traversed any creek he came across and flagged it with red ribbon. When the flagging was done, the green-and-brown grove was lit up with flashes of foreign colour.

As Cronin waded through the thigh-high undergrowth, something caught his eye: a Douglas fir, larger than the rest, with a trunk so wide he could have hidden his truck behind it. He scrambled up the mound of sloughed bark and dead needles that had accumulated around the base of the giant tree.

Dennis Cronin looked up.

The tree dominated the forest—a monarch of its species. Its crown of dark green, glossy needles flitted in the breeze well above the canopy of the forest. Like many of the oldest Douglas firs he had come across in his career, the tree's trunk was limbless until a great height. The species often loses the lower branches that grow in the shadow of the forest's canopy. Many of these large and old Douglas firs have clear marks of disease, with trunks that are twisted and gnarled. This tree's trunk sported few knots and a grain that appeared straight: it was a wonderful specimen of timber, Cronin thought.

With his hand-held hypsometer, a device to measure a standing tree's height using a triangulation of measurements, Cronin took readings from the base and the top of the tree and estimated its stature at approximately seventy metres—around the height of a twenty-storey apartment building. Using a tape, he measured the tree's circumference at 11.91 metres, and calculated the diameter to be 3.79 metres; if felled and loaded onto a train, the log would be wider than an oil tank car. The tree appeared just shy of the Red Creek Fir, the largest Douglas fir in the world, located a couple of valleys away. Cronin didn't know it then, but he had not only stumbled upon one of the largest trees he had ever seen in his career—he had found one of the largest trees in the country. It was surely ancient as well, Cronin knew. A Douglas fir of such height and girth, growing in a wet valley bottom on Vancouver Island, could easily prove half a millennium in age. But to the experienced forester, this one looked much older. *A thousand years?* he wondered.

The logger could have moved on. He could have brushed his broad shoulders past yet another broad trunk and continued through the forest, leaving the giant fir to its fate. He could have walked through the undergrowth, across log and stream, to finish the job of mapping and flagging the cutblock. Fallers would have arrived; the tree would have been brought down in a thunderclap heard kilometres away, hauled from the valley, loaded onto logging trucks, and taken to a mill to be broken down into its most useful and most valuable parts.

Over forty years working on timber hauling crews and as a forest engineer, Cronin had accrued countless days working in the forests of Vancouver Island—he had encountered thousands of enormous trees over his career. But under this one, he lingered. He walked around its circumference, running his hand along the tree's rough and corky bark. He looked up at a trunk so broad and straight it would hold some of the finest and most valued timber on the coast.

Instead of moving on, Cronin reached into his vest pocket for a ribbon he rarely used, tore off a long strip, and wrapped it around the base of the Douglas fir's trunk. The tape wasn't pink or orange or red but green, and along its length were the words "LEAVE TREE."

CHAPTER 2

Evergreen

THE WESTERN COASTLINE OF Vancouver Island ripples like the scalloped blade of a serrated knife, with hundreds of bays, harbours, and estuaries plunging deep into the island. Along the outermost fringe of the craggy shoreline, precariously perched on rocky points, little trees eke out an existence with roots in a crack of soil, bearing the full brunt of the near-constant lashing of storms off the Pacific Ocean. They cling to a life that never allows them to realize their full potential. Often, the side of the tree facing the turbulent water is entirely devoid of branches, or the trunk leans back from being relentlessly pushed by wind and spray. Even on a calm, clear day these small trees appear to shy away from the ocean — as if permanently wincing from the punch they know will come.

Behind these stunted specimens grow sentinels that guard their backs—trees both tall and broad, stoically awaiting the coming storms. They benefit from fertile soils, temperate climates, and nourishing rain. When tempests arrive, they do so with relentless force, battering and drenching without respite. But this wall of wood extending from the northern tip of the island to the southern rim endures—as it has for millennia.

Here, seasons aren't marked by sudden changes of colour or temperature; instead they blend together seamlessly and subtly with demarcations disappearing in the mist. Even at the height of summer, while parts of British Columbia's West Coast glisten like a temperate California, the Pacific rim of Vancouver Island can remain enveloped in grey—locals affectionately call the month after July "Fogust." Waves that crash upon this coast don't immediately roll back to hammer it once again but are left vaporized—suspended in the air as thick banks of mist whose hoary tendrils penetrate deep into the forests. As the trees are draped in this damp, dense white, their spiky forms soften into green-blue silhouettes that gradually fade into nothing.

The valleys of Pacific temperate rainforest can feel both Edenically inviting and primordially ominous. There is alluring comfort among these great trees that embraces your presence and softens your footsteps. What lies beyond the curtain of mist and trees are unknowns: great treasures to be found, or great dangers lurking. One of the largest trees in the country could be hidden a few dozen metres away, obscured in the fog, but so could a bear, a cougar, or a wolf. The canopy above disappears into a grey ceiling and the forests begin to appear manageable. Everything feels within reach.

When the conditions are right, this coastline offers a spectacular sight. It is a brilliant culmination of three of the West Coast's most iconic and characteristic elements—sun, fog, and trees—meeting in perfect unison and producing a result that can be as awesome as a fireworks display or as haunting as an aurora borealis. On a cool, misty morning with a warm, clear forecast, the sun will rise behind the shoreline's forest wall as tree branches bifurcate the rays into hundreds of filigreed beams—each one illuminated by the lingering coastal fog—creating a natural laser light show.

While the fog is the texture of this coastline, it is the rain that is the driving force of life. Vancouver Island rises from the Pacific Ocean like the back of a grey whale breaching the surface of the water. Storms brew in the ocean before hammering the island's west coast with wind, enveloping it in fog, and disgorging rain as the systems hit the Vancouver Island Ranges, mountains and hills that run like a spine down the island's length. This unsheltered rim can receive more than ten times the annual rainfall of the eastern side of the island—and gives truth to the name Canada's Wet Coast.

Nourished by a near-constant supply of rain and sustained by a climate that rarely peaks above thirty degrees Celsius or dips below minus ten, the forest ecosystem of Vancouver Island is never offered a dormant season. For thousands of years, leading up to the arrival of European settlers, the island continuously produced an unbroken evergreen of tangled forest that filled almost every corner of the 31,285-square-kilometre island, and that formed part of a solid band of Pacific temperate rainforest ecosystem that fringed the northwestern edge of the continent. Half of the world's temperate rainforest grows along the west coast of Canada and the United States, from Alaska in the north, through British Columbia, and ending in northern California. The rest is found in small pockets around the world, in countries including Norway, Chile, Ireland, Japan, and New Zealand.

While "Pacific temperate rainforest" is a designation recognized by international organizations such as the World Wildlife Fund, for forest and wildlife management purposes British Columbia has separated itself into fourteen biogeoclimatic zones—depending on a region's climate, geography, and natural characteristics—since 1976. These include the higher-altitude Alpine Tundra zone, the interior Sub-Boreal Spruce zone, and the rare Coastal Douglas Fir zone, found in small pockets of Vancouver Island and mainland B.C. Most of the coastal regions of the province from Haida Gwaii to Victoria fall into the Coastal Western Hemlock zone—named after the species of tree found most commonly throughout its range. This region is the wettest zone of the entire province, with annual rainfall of up to 4,500 millimetres. Here, mounds of moss growing on tree branches twenty storeys high hold moisture long after rains have ceased. Even when the sun has taken the place of the clouds, water can still fall like rain in these forests. Nearly the entirety of Vancouver Island is in the Coastal Western Hemlock zone, with the exception of patches of higher-elevation alpine regions and a thin band of a Coastal Douglas Fir zone that runs along the southeastern coast down to Victoria. It is here that the trees, when left for centuries, can achieve truly tremendous growth—wider than an SUV is long, and taller than two blue whales stacked nose to tail.

THE WORDS "OLD-GROWTH FOREST" evoke a Tolkienesque grove of trunk-to-trunk behemoths separated by flat patches of easily traversable mossy ground. But in Pacific temperate rainforests, like those found on Vancouver Island, the reality is much more complex.

There is no order in these forests: trees of every size and age grow here, and windfall litters the ground in various stages of decomposition. Under a canopy of dark green foliage, thick salal bushes make one section impenetrable to pedestrians, next to another that opens into a small clearing. Some trees appear painted in moss, while grey lichen known colloquially as "old man's beard" droops from branches of the older trees like tinsel left long after Christmas. The largest trees pierce the canopy, allowing long beams of light to penetrate the forest floor.

The term "old growth" had been used casually by forestry professionals in British Columbia's timber industry throughout the twentieth century. But in the 1970s, it began to be employed by ecologists and scientists as a loose definition of any forest undisturbed by significant human impact. Predominantly, the definition has come to encapsulate any forest untouched by commercial logging. But while historical signs of human impact within these forests are less obvious than a clear-cut, these ecosystems do show the scars of human presence. Before the arrival of European settlers, Vancouver Island's forests were not "untouched" or "unspoilt" landscapes, as they are often referred to. For as long as there have been humans on the island, trees have been felled, bark harvested, and innumerable aspects of the forests used.

More than fifty First Nations have inhabited the island, collectively in three Indigenous peoples: the

Kwakwaka'wakw to the north, the Coast Salish to the south, and the Nuu'chah'nulth along the west-central coast of the island. There are dozens of nations among them. Along the coast, many of the larger nations, each with populations numbering in the thousands, became fragmented after a great flood in 1700—the result of a cataclysmic earthquake and tsunami that forced salt water nearly half a kilometre inland. Along the island's southwest coast, one nation—the Pacheedaht, or the "people of the sea foam"—rebuilt at two estuary sites around the mouth of the Diitiida River, also now known as the Jordan River, and within a large bay that centuries later would be named Port San Juan by Spanish colonialists. Throughout the twentieth century, as development and industry—mining, logging, and hydroelectric operations—increased around the Jordan River, the Pacheedaht saw the salmon stocks, which would run up the river to spawn every fall, begin to dwindle. The volume of fish became so depleted that the Diitiida community relocated north up the coast, to the head of Port San Juan.

The Pacheedaht can trace their history along this coastline for millennia. Their recorded presence is more often found not by uncovering anything constructed—houses eventually crumble and rot away—but within the region's forests, within the very trees themselves that bear the scars of harvesting or logging. Wherever patches of Pacific temperate rainforest grow, archaeological evidence of the Indigenous population can be found. On Vancouver Island, these marks—a strip of bark peeled from a live trunk; a "window" carved into a tree to test its solidity for canoe building; an entire plank removed from the side of a tree—are most commonly found in western red cedars. These culturally modified trees (CMTS), as they are known, bear evidence of procedures that were done carefully, to remove a part of the tree without killing it, and have been documented across the island—on mountainsides and in valleys, along the coast and in the interior—and provide clues about how forests were used before the arrival of European settlers. Many archaeological finds, be they a fragment of pottery or a stone wall, point to a vague date range, a decade or two at best, but a CMT can offer a specificity of age down to the year, simply by a researcher counting the rings of the tree.

In 1996, the British Columbia government issued a directive regulating how culturally modified trees should be handled and protected: any site that predates 1846 is protected under the Heritage Conservation Act. In 2001, a logger named George Halpert was the first person charged with cutting down protected CMTS—the trees, located near Terrace, British Columbia, dated back to the 1600s. He was sentenced to six months' probation and required to make a formal apology to the Kitsumkalum First Nation.

When CMTs are found, often by timber workers, they must be recorded in their company site plans and the local First Nation notified, but CMTs dating to after 1846 hold no formal protection. Often, timber companies incorporate them in a riparian area—a buffer of trees left standing around a river, lake, or wetland—and exclude the historic trees from their cutting plan. The company must apply for a permit to alter the site plan if they want to cut down the CMT, which has to be agreed upon by the First Nation. But a First Nation's desire to understand its past can supersede the push to preserve every tree possible. A CMT left standing can only offer so much. It can show how a bark strip was cut away from a cedar to be turned into baskets or clothing. It can show how Indigenous peoples probed a live tree to determine whether or not it was fit to be turned into a canoe. But a felled tree can reveal much more. A cut log can be accurately dated through its rings, to reveal new information about the age, scope, or reach of a First Nation. In particular, was the CMT pre-contact or post-contact?

In a forest south of Port Renfrew, the Pacheedaht culturally modified tree crew, which works in conjunction with regional timber companies, found 180 CMTs within a single thirty-hectare patch. The density was surprising, but it was the location—far inland from the seaside hamlet of Jordan River—that helped redefine the nation's understanding of their historical range.

Culturally modified trees are as much a part of an old-growth forest as any great tree that has been left unmolested to grow for hundreds of years or any grove that has remained predominantly undisturbed by human impact. Rather than being "original" or "untouched" or "virgin," as these forests are often described, old-growth forests are complete, and every stage of growth—from seedling to skyscraper—is represented.

Old-growth forests can be found across Canada—in the stubby spruces of the Maritimes, in the vast expanse of the northern boreal, and in the squat, high-altitude stands of the Rocky Mountains. The term can be appropriately applied to each forest, despite the radical differences in appearance. Even within Vancouver Island, forests that are considered old growth range from scraggly stands clinging to a mountainside to stunted forests growing out of bogs—as well as the more identifiable, high-productivity valleys that produce the country's biggest trees. The size of a grove's trees is not the principal factor in an old-growth forest.

In drier climates, forests are kept youthful by fire that constantly scrapes the land clear and creates a blank slate for new growth. But along the western half of Vancouver Island, in the lee of the interior mountains, plunging valleys of deep green are rarely touched by the ravages of fire. Compared to the interior of the province, or even the eastern side of the island, lightning doesn't present much of a threat. There are groves that have never seen fire in their entire existence—ever since tree seedlings first sprouted out of glacial sediment as the last ice age retreated northwards around twelve thousand years ago.

Without the refreshing cleanse of fire, the forests in these wet valleys are allowed to continuously grow with little disturbance. As a result, Pacific temperate rainforests hold the largest biomass—the total amount of flora and fauna, alive and dead—of any ecosystem on the planet. They even hold more biomass than forests found in the tropics, where the greater heat breaks down dead matter more quickly, in a rapid churn from life to death to life again. But in the rainforests of Vancouver Island, this cycle is decelerated—a fallen cedar log will gradually decompose, but can remain virtually intact for well over a century—and biomass is allowed to accumulate. Each discernible characteristic of an old-growth forest—the biodiversity, the complexity of structure, the presence of both live and dead matter—is a product of a singular unhalting force: time.

In British Columbia's drier interior, a forest is considered old growth when it is more than approximately 150 years old. On the province's coast and islands, it is when a forest is more than 250 years old. But apart from age, neither the province of British Columbia nor timber companies have agreed upon a formal and universally accepted definition of what constitutes an old-growth forest. Various ecosystems around the province, and indeed the country, may satisfy the age requirement but look wholly different whether found in the wet valleys of western Vancouver Island or in the high-elevation coastal mountains or in the dry interior.

Timber companies have used this imprecision to their advantage. They often speak of forests that have partially succumbed to the destructive natural forces of fire or wind within the 250-year window not as an "old-growth forest" but as a forest that may hold "old-growth characteristics," with several "veteran trees." It is a classification that suits their purposes: they aren't cutting tracts of old-growth forest, it is often presented; they are cutting younger, second-growth stands with a handful of old-growth trees.

Clear definitions are crucial, for both environmental activists trying to protect this precarious ecosystem and timber companies trying to extract hard value from it. Monitoring deforestation is challenging when parameters and interpretations vary between local organizations and companies, and also around the world. On a global scale, according to the United Nations Framework Convention on Climate Change, what constitutes a forest can include an ecosystem with as low as 10 percent tree cover. There exist more than eight hundred definitions of "forest," based upon a number of factors, including location, climate, temperature, soil condition, and the presence of human activity. On a local scale, the lack of a clear definition and set of parameters means environmental groups argue that there is very little old-growth forest left, while timber companies maintain that there is plenty, by including old-growth forests growing in bogs or in high-alpine regions, where trees are often stunted and difficult to access and are therefore of little timber value. Environmental activists become frustrated with this inclusion. To them, the immediate focus lies on the high-productivity areas that offer the most ideal conditions for trees to grow big. There lies a different kind of value: one that can be extracted not in terms of cubic metres of cut timber but in terms of cultural, social, and environmental returns.

ON THE FLOOR OF Vancouver Island's old-growth forests, life teems in every square metre. One researcher calculated that when he goes walking in these coastal forests, eighteen thousand invertebrates wriggle within the column of soil under each step of his size 9.5 shoes. In this verdant and lively layer, sword ferns erupt out of the damp, peaty earth as curly fiddleheads, before growing into waist-high thickets of bracken. Salmonberry bushes form tangled and impenetrable walls, while delicate huckleberries sprout from moss-covered trunks. Mushrooms unfurl overnight, revealing caps as pure white as fresh snow or as glossy black as obsidian. Among it all, black bears bound through the bush to make their dens in hollow trees, while elk rub their antlers against the tree trunks and deer nibble on new shoots. Squirrels and chipmunks drop detritus from snacking on seeds into piles on the forest floor. And above, great trees grow so large they block out the sun. The rainforests of Vancouver Island are one of the few environments on the planet that hold some of the world's biggest trees alongside large carnivores including mountain lions, wolves, and bears, and ungulates such as elk and deer. These forests are home to species that depend entirely on ancient characteristics. The marbled murrelet, a seabird that migrates along the coast, doesn't nest on cliffs but builds them out of lichen and moss in the very tops of old-growth trees—often only on Douglas firs that are more than 150 years old. The Queen Charlotte goshawk, a yellow- or red-eyed raptor, lives and nests in older forests along the coast from Vancouver Island to Haida Gwaii—and typically in the tallest trees. The hawk is classified as "threatened" under the federal Species at Risk Act, whose registry states that "continued logging of low-elevation, old growth coniferous forest" is the bird's most significant danger to its survival.

But this ecosystem is not defined by its black bears or elk, nor its tens of thousands of species of invertebrates, insects, and birds. These are forests, after all, where every aspect—the nourishing rain, the moderate seasons, and the supporting biomass—contributes to the gargantuan growth of this environment's signature feature. The western red cedar, the Sitka spruce, the Douglas fir—within this ecosystem, these trees grow not just voraciously but continuously, into the planet's largest expressions of their respective species. The tallest Douglas fir ever measured anywhere in the world was a 126.5-metre behemoth—the size of one and a quarter football fields—found in 1902 in Lynn Valley, on the North Shore of Vancouver. To encounter a great tree in a forest, one that is three metres in diameter and a hundred metres tall, is to come face to face with one of nature's grandest creations.

There are few things on the planet that have been growing and thriving for a millennium. To some, stepping into an ancient forest can evoke a sense of religious or spiritual awe, as if entering a church or mosque or temple—columns replaced with trunks, marble floors and pews with soft soil and leafy undergrowth, and altars with trees. Old-growth Pacific temperate rainforests are cathedrals of nature, awesome in their grandeur and yet humbling in their structure. Throughout history, such aged forests have represented something dark and mysterious, dangerous and unknown.

But individual trees have always held an allure that provokes curiosity. They have been sources of wonder and magic, and of perceived wisdom through age. To see and touch these ancient trees is to confront centuries of history, technological progress, and social and cultural evolution—the light and the dark of human development. To stand next to a tree that has withstood everything nature and humans have thrown at it—fire, storm, industry, climate change—is to be reminded of our capacity to nurture as well as our capacity to destroy. To be dwarfed by a tree that would dominate most city blocks is to have any form of hubris quashed.

Hemlocks, ubiquitous and opportunistic, sprout out of a dead log seemingly the hour after it falls to the forest floor. They grow ready and able to survive and thrive in nearly any condition, filling in the gaps. While not the most outwardly grand, they are sturdy and applicable, recognizable by their delicate tops that arch over as if bowing subserviently to the larger trees. Among the conifers grow the odd deciduous trees: alders, often the first to regrow in a clear-cut, spring up to attention like a company of soldiers with their spear-shaped leaves; and the colourful and colour-shifting maples ignite the green with flashes of fire and movement. Magnanimous and regal at the top are three species that make these forests Brobdingnagian in scale. A grove of Sitka spruces, with their columnar trunks and finely scaled bark, grow into natural pillars as true as any stonemason's creation. Cedars, sporting their multi-pronged crowns and fine bark, conceal warm-coloured wood, ready to be transformed into boats, baskets, building materials, and instruments. And Douglas firs, with their wide and hulking trunks, cracked bark, and dominant forms, protrude through the canopy like towers.

For millennia, the Indigenous people on Vancouver Island have held the cedar in exalted status. They used the versatile tree—in its yellow and western red species—in innumerable ways. They split its bark and wove it into baskets and clothing; they harnessed the wood's flexibility and steamed it into boxes and containers so tightly fitted they could hold water; and they sought out the prime specimens with which to build houses and carve canoes. A single tree, with its light and rot-resistant wood, could produce products that spanned a spectrum of uses.

The eighteenth- and nineteenth-century British settlers arrived with a more brutish approach. They brought with them smallpox, which wiped out nearly a third of the province's Indigenous population, and they brought people to build towns and cities, as well as a view that forests were to be managed, nature was to be controlled, and the wild was to be tamed. This view was reflected not in the soft and malleable wood of the cedar, but in the hard and sturdy wood of another tree. While this tree could be found across the province, it was along the coasts and on the islands where it achieved the pinnacle of its growth. Since its inception, around the middle of the nineteenth century, British Columbia's commercial timber industry has been dominated by one species, the tree of a thousand uses: the Douglas fir.

CHAPTER 3

A Tree of Many Names

ON MARCH 29, 1778, Captain James Cook sailed his ships, HMS *Resolution* and HMS *Discovery*, into a broad inlet two-thirds up the west coast of Vancouver Island. The region would come to be known as Nootka Sound, based off either an anglicization of Nuu'chah'nulth, the name for the local First Nation, or from an Indigenous word meaning to "go around." The mountain Cook had seen at the head of the inlet was in fact a large island. The British vessels were in need of repairs, with broken masts and spars from their crossing of the Pacific via Hawaii, known then as the Sandwich Islands. The crew immediately went ashore in search of timber.

"I raised my eyes to the sky and could see nothing but the worthless timber that covered everything," one

British man remarked. Furs were the primary target, highly prized for their low weight and high value—as ships began to be used not only to transport explorers but also to return with valuable commodities in their holds—but it wasn't long before expedition financiers began to see value in the endless forests. Timber could be strapped to the deck of a ship and fetch a significant price in places like Western Europe, where trees of the magnitude found on Vancouver Island were the stuff of legend. When British captain and fur trader John Meares left Nootka Sound in 1788 with a ship laden with raw timbers, he remarked, "Indeed the woods of this part of America are capable of supplying, with these valuable materials, all the navies of Europe."

After several decades of burgeoning colonial settlement along the coast, in the spring of 1825 the Hudson's Bay Company ship *William and Ann* sailed into the mouth of the Columbia River, the largest river that spills into the Pacific Ocean, located in modern-day Washington state. The vessel had left England nine months prior with a mission to resupply the forts and trading posts along this coast, one of the most remote corners of the company's expansion. On board, a man named David Douglas gazed across the tranquil waters to the impenetrable-looking forests that fringed the riverbanks. There lay trees taller and larger than any he had seen in his career as a budding botanist.

His mission was simple in its goal but challenging in practice. A year before leaving England, Douglas had quit his job as gardener at the Glasgow Botanic Garden to accept a position at the Horticultural Society of London. Established in 1804, the society was beginning to expand and form a mandate: to promote the study, discussion, and discovery of new plant species. The society's burgeoning gardens had been created by the samples that had been collected by roving botanists sent around the world. There, in his first year tending the gardens, Douglas mastered the care of plants and trees and began pushing himself to learn more experimental techniques in breeding, cloning, and propagation. But Douglas had grown up tramping the highlands and moors around his hometown of Scone, Scotland, and his ambition could not be contained to the orderliness of a city. He set his sights on one of the coveted positions of "society explorer," a post that would allow him to leave the greenhouse and garden. These intrepid envoys were dispatched on botanizing expeditions to document previously unknown species of plant growing in the farthest reaches of the British Empire—South Asia, East Africa, the Far East, Australia, and the Americas. They returned with drawings, paintings, and descriptions that delighted and enthralled naturalists. More important to the society, however, was to return, if possible, with not just drawings but samples—seeds that could be sown and nurtured in the greenhouses of London, and eventually studied, classified, and propagated.

With glowing recommendations from some of the field's most respected members, Douglas was deemed by the Horticultural Society a keen and ideal candidate to join a ship to the northwest coast of North America. The society bestowed on him an ambitious assignment: after acquiring a brief taste of the natural bounty that grew along this coastline—unusual flowers and trees of unimaginable heights—it now needed to confirm the documentation of species amassed on previous expeditions that it held in its archives. For an experienced botanist, collecting plants and seeds in a location like the west coast of North America was relatively simple, especially for a Scot working in a familiar climate. This was not the humid tropics, after all. But ensuring the survival of the samples during the three-month return voyage around Cape Horn to England was a complicated gamble. Months, if not years, of work could be destroyed in an instant. Moisture meant ruin, so samples, cones, and seeds were kept as dry as possible in order to stave off rot or mould. In one doomed instance, another Scottish botanist, Robert Fortune, had laboured over the collection of tea seeds from deep in China's interior. But his specimens, which he had planted in glass terrariums known as Wardian cases, were ruined after being opened upon arrival in muggy Calcutta, India, rather than the cool climate of hilly Bengal, which would have been similar to their origin. He had to replicate the whole ordeal before the plantations in Darjeeling could be started—and eventually produce world-famous tea.

The European botanizing missions of the late eighteenth and early nineteenth centuries weren't purely scientific—sending out seemingly benign botanists into the forests and fields was also the act of a colonizer. David Douglas's job was to accurately describe the terrain and its potential—floral, faunal, and mineral—for the advancement of science as well as for the possible development of resource extraction. Along this northwest coast of North America, the borders between British, American, and Spanish conquest were just being drawn—erasing those that had been adhered to by Indigenous people for centuries—and the wealth that lay both below and above ground was beginning to be realized.

As Douglas sailed up the Columbia River, he was overwhelmed with excitement at the possibilities on offer. "The scenery," Douglas wrote in his journal, "round this place is sublimely grand—lofty, well-wooded hills, mountains covered with perpetual snow, extensive natural meadows, and plains of deep, fertile, alluvial deposit, covered with a rich sward of grass, and a profusion of flowering plants." On his botanizing missions he travelled throughout the Columbia region, which covered what is now northern Washington State and southern British Columbia, with near free rein.

Within six months of landing, Douglas had collected 499 species of flora, which he pressed and dried between sheets of paper and described in remarkable detail in his journal. For the species that were known to the botanists of the Horticultural Society, he added more detail or more accurate information. But many he documented were hitherto unknown to British botanists, including some species that are now iconic of the natural landscape of the North American coast, like the orange California poppy and several species of the multicoloured lupin; and shrubs such as salal, ocean spray, and Oregon grape. But it was the trees—including the peely-barked arbutus and the columnar Sitka spruce—that fascinated him deeply, in this land of never-ending giants.

When the *William and Ann* embarked on its return journey to England, within her hull were boxes and crates of Douglas's acquisitions: sixteen large bundles of dried plants, as well as preserved samples of birds and mammals. But the most significant chest contained more than a hundred varieties of seeds. The Scottish botanist was also a cautious man—he retained a small collection of seeds from some of his most prized species, which he intended to carry personally by land across North America as a precautionary measure in case the ship was lost at sea. He sent so many conifer seeds and samples back to England that he remarked to William Jackson Hooker, his mentor at the Horticultural Society, "You will begin to think that I manufacture pines at my pleasure."

Some of the species David Douglas encountered were uncommon, like the purple wild hyacinth, and some otherworldly, like the sequoia—the tallest tree species in the world. While Douglas undoubtedly came across specimens of this species that were taller than any building in existence anywhere around the world, he returned time and again to another species of tree that he encountered throughout his travels and that grew in great quantities and to great heights—a large conifer with thick bark and dark green needles. It was a tree that the botanist would be best known for, and would eventually colloquially bear his name: the Douglas fir.

He found the species growing in the two most common climates of this region: along the wet coasts and throughout the drier inland hills:

> The trees which are interspersed in groups or standing solitary in dry, upland, thin, gravelly soils or on rocky situations, are thickly clad to the very ground with widespreading pendent

> branches, and from the gigantic size which they attain in such places and from the compact habit uniformly preserved they form one of the most striking and truly graceful objects in Nature. Those on the other hand which are in the dense gloomy forests, two-thirds of which are composed of this species, are more than usually straight, the trunks being destitute of branches to the height of 100 to 140 feet, being in many places so close together that they naturally prune themselves, and in the almost impenetrable parts where they stand at an average distance of five square feet, they frequently attain greater height... In such places some arrive at a magnitude exceeded by few if any trees in the world...

Douglas described one sixty-nine-metre-tall specimen he came across—one that he remarked was exemplary for its girth: 14.6 metres in circumference at its base. While walking in the fir forests that surrounded Mount St. Helens, in modern-day Washington State, Douglas noted: "A forest of these trees is a spectacle too much for one man to see."

The collecting of cones from this tree proved difficult, due to its great height and lack of low branches. As a botanist, Douglas was unequipped to fell such a tree—or even one much smaller than the one he stood before—possessing neither the equipment (he carried only a small hatchet) nor the will to climb one. He tried using his gun to shoot at the high branches in an attempt to dislodge a cone, but the buckshot he had brought for hunting birds and ducks proved ineffective. He resigned himself to collecting cones from much smaller examples of the species.

But while the specimens Douglas encountered along the Columbia River were grand, the ideal climate for the tree was farther north—in the wet, lush rainforests of Vancouver Island, where the species had first been documented by another Scottish man. Botanist Archibald Menzies had tracked the island's forests—first in 1786 with the crew of the *Prince of Wales* and again in 1792 under the captainship of George Vancouver aboard the *Discovery*. Near Nootka Sound, Menzies traversed Vancouver Island collecting samples of tree, flower, and plant. He described in his journal and collected seeds from one tree previously unknown to botanists in Britain. But the seeds Menzies sent to London never arrived; it wasn't until April 1826 that the first samples and seeds of this great conifer, sent by David Douglas, were successfully delivered to the Horticultural Society of London.

Douglas returned to England in October 1827, but after two years, he boarded another ship and returned to the Columbia River. In all, he set a record for the most species ever introduced by a society explorer.

"The botanical world was literally startled by the number and importance of his discoveries," wrote a biographer. He was admitted to the Linnean Society, the Zoological Society of London, and the Geological Society of London.

On January 1, 1826, during his first visit to the northwest, Douglas wrote in his journal:

> Commencing a year in such a far removed corner of the earth, where I am nearly destitute of civilized society, there is some scope for reflection. In 1824, I was on the Atlantic on my way to England; 1825, between the island of Juan Fernandez and the Galapagos in the Pacific; I am now here, and God only knows where I may be next. In all probability, if a change does not take place, I will shortly be consigned to the tomb. I can die satisfied with myself. I never have given cause for remonstrance or pain to an individual on earth. I am in my 27th year.

David Douglas died eight years later, on June 12, 1834, while hiking a volcano in Hawaii in search of new plants.

A coastal Douglas fir, originally from the west coast of North America, is now the tallest conifer in Europe. The tallest tree growing anywhere in the United Kingdom is a Douglas fir that was planted in the 1880s in Reelig Glen, a grove in Scotland that lies two and a half hours from the birthplace of David Douglas.

FOR NEARLY TWO HUNDRED YEARS, what is now commonly called the Douglas fir held numerous taxonomic names. In the early 1800s, years after Archibald Menzies had sent back drawings and descriptions to Britain, the tree was classified as a pine and given the name *Pinus taxifolia*. Throughout the nineteenth century, the tree was bounced from classification to classification, including *Abies* as a fir, *Tsuga* as a hemlock, and *Pinus* as a pine. During the expeditions of David Douglas in the 1820s and '30s, the tree went by several names, including *Pinus douglasii*—which Douglas himself used in his journals, a bit self-servingly. While his name didn't stick, the specimens Douglas collected and shipped back to the Horticultural Society of London helped reveal a surprise about the tree—that the Douglas fir, the king of the firs, was not really a fir at all.

In 1867, it was proposed to rename the tree *Pseudotsuga douglasii*—*pseudo*, Greek for "false," and *tsuga*, Japanese for "hemlock"—to mark that, nearly eight decades after it was first documented, the tree had been found to be an imposter that had fooled many early botanists. (Today, the tree is often written hyphenated, Douglas-fir, as a signal of its outlier status.) The tree's cones hung below its needled branches, unlike those of true firs which stand above.

The species stands as an example of the trials and uncertainties of taxonomy. The confusion may have arisen because the Douglas fir appeared to have several varieties. At higher elevations and in rockier soils, the tree grows to a considerably more stunted version than the gargantuan specimens found in damp valley bottoms. Along the coasts, salt-laden spray and air tinges the tree's needles a noticeably bluer hue than those trees that grow away from the ocean, which appear as a truer dark green. The smell of the foliage of those found in dense, lush valleys has a distinct citrus tone; whereas those that grow closer to the sea or on more exposed hillsides offer a more pungent, turpentine odour. These inconsistencies, among others, confused botanists and taxonomists for decades.

In 1892, the *Journal of the Royal Horticultural Society* highlighted the complicated issue of taxonomic naming with regards to David Douglas's work in documenting the Douglas fir:

> It is unfortunate, and it seems unjust, that the discoverer of an object in natural history—one who, like Douglas, has the energy and daring to explore, the intelligence to comprehend when he has an object in sight that is new to science, and,

> moreover, the ability to describe and name it correctly, referring it to the proper genus in vogue at the time of publishing—it seems unjust that such a namer should subsequently lose the honours of discovery and of authorship, because, forsooth, another view of the relative importance of groups places the object in another category, and therefore another person, to wit, the one who so places it, becomes the author of the species. Such is the latest usage, however, based upon lately revived ancient laws of nomenclature; and, in the long run, it works less mischief than would a reverse rule, whereby pseudo-scientists could air their vanity by foisting upon us a host of unfounded terms at will.

In 1950, David Douglas and his work to help classify the species was officially stripped of recognition. The tree was renamed *Pseudotsuga menziesii* in honour of Archibald Menzies, who had been the first European botanist to document the tree when he encountered it on Vancouver Island.

Still, in the end Douglas came out on top, in perhaps what matters most: vernacular rather than technical usage. At times, the tree has been colloquially called Oregon pine or red fir, but most people today know of the species by one name: the Douglas fir—the fir of Douglas.

VARIOUS LARGE TREES DOMINATE the forests of Vancouver Island—western red cedars, Sitka spruces, bigleaf maples, western and mountain hemlocks—but the Douglas fir is the grand, albeit humble, icon of coastal British Columbia. Douglas firs can be found in B.C. in two regions, with geography and climates producing variations among the species. In the province's interior, the drier environment produces trees that are stubbier and shorter, appearing in a more classic Christmas tree form, with branches of needles growing from near the base to the very top. This variation is more resistant to frost and cold, as temperatures in the Rocky Mountains often dip well below freezing.

Along the province's coast, by contrast, grows a variety of Douglas fir that thrives in wetter environments such as the deep and damp valleys of Vancouver Island. Because of the density of these forests, the older examples of coastal Douglas firs often shed their lower branches below the forest's canopy level, creating a clean trunk with a crown of branches and needles and resembling a Corinthian column. The combination of more stable climates, plentiful rainfall, and nutrient-rich soils produces specimens of more than double the size of their interior cousins. It is along the coastline and on the islands of British Columbia that the Douglas fir earns its place as one of the largest trees in North America, with historical records of some pushing forty storeys tall.

In 1895, a logger named George Cary felled a gargantuan Douglas fir outside Vancouver. The tree was said to have been nearly 8 metres in diameter at its base and 127 metres tall—about one-quarter the height of Toronto's CN Tower. The Cary Fir, as it became known, remained little more than a story of great accomplishment told among timber workers—for bringing down a tree of such proportions quickly became lore. Then, in 1922, a photograph supposedly of the legendary fir graced the August cover of *Western Lumberman*. The image depicted an enormous log lying on its side, upon which six men, two women, six children, and a baby sat or stood. One man balanced on the sixth rung of a ladder leaning up against the log—apparently George Cary—was still several metres from reaching the top.

After publication, however, doubts were raised as to the authenticity of the photograph. Some claim the image is not of a Douglas fir but of a coast redwood, commonly known as a sequoia. Many of these ochre-coloured giants are located in Redwood National Park in northern California—including Hyperion, the tallest living tree in the world at more than 115 metres in height. But foresters and experts were uncertain, and the debate about the species of the photographed tree raged, to no universally agreed-upon conclusion. Ecologists and silviculturists also disagreed on whether the standing trees behind the log appear to be that of a Douglas fir forest found along British Columbia's coast or of a forest found in northern California.

Rumours also bubbled that the image was simply a fake, created by superimposing out-of-scale human figures onto a photograph of a large log, and used as a tool by British Columbian businessmen to lure American investors to their province's timber ventures — an attempt at manipulation akin to evoking a nineteenth-century "strike it rich" frenzy with an image of someone holding a gold-painted rock the size of a grapefruit and calling it a nugget. However, experts have concluded that period technology in image manipulation would have been detectable. The source of the image remains a mystery, but the story, to many, was plausible. There are countless other trees of truly tremendous heights — well documented with photographs and anecdotes — that had been felled, having grown in ideal conditions in the valley bottoms of coastal British Columbia.

Despite being moved by the scale, grandeur, and uniformity of the large conifer that would bear his name, David Douglas also recognized that underneath the thick bark was immense value.

"The wood," he wrote in his journal, "may be found very useful for a variety of domestic purposes: the young slender ones exceedingly well adapted for making ladders and scaffold poles, not being liable to cast;

the larger timber for more important purposes; while at the same time the rosin [resin] may be found deserving attention."

In the winter of 1847, tests were conducted in the dockyard of Portsmouth, on the south coast of England, to determine if the Douglas fir logs from Vancouver Island were stronger and better-suited as spars than those that shipbuilders had been importing from the shores of the Baltic Sea. The North American fir proved superior, and the British Admiralty placed an order paying up to a hundred pounds (around $12,000 today) for a single twenty-one-metre log, sixty centimetres in diameter.

Throughout the nineteenth century, the Douglas fir was prized by the settlers who built along the western Canadian and American coast. In his 1918 book, *Steep Trails*, the Scottish-American naturalist John Muir, renowned environmentalist and father of the U.S. National Parks, praised the species as "tough and durable and admirably adapted in every way for shipbuilding, piles, and heavy timbers." Loggers and millers found the wood dimensionally stable—it doesn't twist or warp when drying—while consumers prized its pronounced grain and warm colour, which made it ideal for flooring, doors, windows, and beams. Because of its resistance to fire, the timber was advertised to early twentieth century builders as preferable to steel, which would bend and buckle. The Douglas fir, by contrast, would char but remain intact. Many living veterans of the species bear the black scars of a fire that once raged through the forest.

Streets were even paved with Douglas fir. Over the course of the nineteenth century, roads in towns and cities from Victoria to San Francisco were laid with wooden planks. In 1908, Waddington Alley—a narrow passageway connecting Yates and Johnson Streets in downtown Victoria—was paved with creosote-soaked blocks of Douglas fir, stacked with its strong edge-grain facing upwards. The alley underwent a full renovation in 1992, and continues to be maintained with wooden cobbles from Douglas fir trees harvested on Vancouver Island.

The species grew to such iconic status that at Expo 67, the World's Fair held in Montreal in Canada's centenary year, the Western Provinces pavilion featured Douglas fir trees so tall their tops protruded out of the roof of the structure. Visitors passed under their branches and around a genuine logging truck fully loaded with wood, while sounds of a timber camp—chainsaws, falling trees—played through the speakers.

As British Columbia's logging industry expanded, the species grew to become its number-one resource, with coastal and interior varieties of Douglas fir producing more timber than any other tree in North America.

The coastal Douglas fir ecosystem is one of the most threatened in the country, in the hallowed company of the "Pocket Desert" in British Columbia, the Tall Grass Prairie in Manitoba, and the Carolinian Forest in Ontario. Today, 99 percent of the original Douglas firs on Vancouver Island and British Columbia's south coast have been logged.

CHAPTER 4

Green Gold

WHILE DRIVING THE LOGGING roads offers an intimate portrait of the state of Vancouver Island's forested landscape, the scope of timber harvesting is best realized from the air. Viewed out of a plane window at a thousand feet up, the southern half of Vancouver Island appears as a patchwork quilt, simultaneously ragged and ordered from industrial logging. Some hillsides appear as if shaved by a fifteen-year-old boy with his first razor: small tufts and patches here and there, often in the most inaccessible places. Others are puzzle-like in the uniformity of the clear-cuts. Cutblocks are easily discernible in their various stages of use: freshly cut are orange, recently cut are grey, light green are regrowing, and darker green are re-established.

At first glance, many areas of the island appear covered in trees. But with a keen eye, the reality comes into focus: nearly every tree has been planted by human hands. There's a saying among West Coast ecologists: in a second-growth forest, a deer would have to pack a lunch. There just isn't enough to eat. Even at high noon, a replanted forest is a dark place: the uniform canopy formed by even-aged trees creates a thick barrier that blocks most sunlight from penetrating to the forest floor, resulting in an environment often bare of the substantial and complex undergrowth found in old-growth forests. The biodiversity of plant species is replaced with a monocrop of trees growing closely together and at the exact same rate, in unison, as grass does in a lawn. The complexity of structure is lost without the benefit of time and death. Second-growth forests are grown not to be self-regenerative or as a replacement for original stands—they are grown to be harvested. Every clear-cut will regrow, whether naturally over time or with the assistance of a silviculture program. But many questions remain: What will a regrown 250-year-old forest look like? Will it have the same biodiversity or the same depth of biomass as one never touched by commercial logging? Will it have the same complex structure and interwoven networks? We have yet to arrive at a point where any commercial clear-cut has regrown long enough to tell.

When a patch of boreal — the forest that covers much of Canada's sub-Arctic north — is harvested, what grows back will look relatively similar to its original form in around a century. In West Coast forests, however, estimates project that a replanted cutblock will begin looking as it once did in closer to half a millennium. On Vancouver Island, second-growth forests are allowed to grow for only fifty or sixty years before they are logged once again. For the vast majority of replanted regions, the plan is never to regrow forests like those that once stood.

From the ground or from the air, it takes an even keener eye to see the vestiges of original forest on Vancouver Island. Often, they appear as a small patch at the top of a mountain or down a steep hillside — places more difficult for loggers to access. Provincial parks, with their protected trees, stand out of the landscape like Central Park does in an aerial view of New York City. But if hikers and visitors were to walk towards the edge of a provincial park, they would meet the end of the green. Sky would appear through the trees, and the reality of the extent of forest loss would become shockingly clear as they stepped into a clear-cut.

ON NOVEMBER 24, 1848, a few kilometres west of the fledgling British colony known as Fort Victoria on the southern tip of the island, a waterwheel-powered sawmill began operations. It was the first mill in the territory that nearly a quarter of a century later would become the province of British Columbia. From this Millstream facility, the first commercial shipment of timber ever sent from Vancouver Island across the channel to the mainland reached the Hudson's Bay Company outpost of Langley. In Nanaimo, a hundred kilometres north along the eastern coast of the island, the Hudson's Bay Company opened a second mill in 1854. While most of the mill's logs were cut by settlers, some were traded by local Indigenous communities. At that time, eight logs—each four and a half metres long, and forty centimetres in diameter at the narrow end—would fetch one Hudson's Bay blanket. The most famous mill was the Anderson sawmill opened by Captain Edward Stamp, a British lumberman, in 1861 along the Alberni Inlet. Within its first year, it was producing fourteen thousand board feet (a unit of measuring timber, twelve inches by twelve inches by one inch thick) of lumber every day, which was being shipped as far abroad as Australia and Peru.

But it was the discovery of gold that ignited the region's timber trade. Stories of riches in the Cariboo in the Fraser Valley during the late 1850s, and in the Yukon's Klondike region in the final years of the century, fuelled the need for timber in order to turn backwater outposts and fledgling colonies into bustling towns with general stores, saloons, and hotels in support of the prospectors going north.

When word of the initial discoveries of gold along the North American coast crossed the Atlantic, British botanists at the Horticultural Society of London remembered something they had seen in a shipment of trees they had received years prior. When they examined the collection of pines from California that David Douglas had sent, within each sample's bundled-up mass of root and soil were flakes of gold.

At the time, the London botanists who received Douglas's samples had ignored the glittering flakes tangled in the roots of the seedlings. They weren't interested in the potential riches that they could have exploited years before prospectors flooded the river valleys. Instead, they saw value in the fragile seeds and seedlings they held in their hands. But as the California Gold Rush grew, and news of the riches being earned began to circulate, both the botanists who had been in the field and their colleagues back in England who had received the gold-laden samples seventeen years prior became the target of blame. Their omission is understandable, considering small samples of gold had been uncovered across California throughout the decades leading up to the 1848 rush. Still, the oversight shows how focused these men were on floral rather than mineral discoveries; they couldn't even be distracted from their goals by the most glittering and beguiling of natural treasures.

And it's unlikely Douglas himself realized the magnitude of his discovery when he was making his collections—whether he deemed his accidental mineral-finding insignificant or whether he was simply too preoccupied with documenting new species of tree and flower. His journals are noticeably absent of mentions of hitting pay dirt of that kind. Naturalist explorers of his ilk and era were discouraged from scouring the creeks, rivers, and caves for gold; they were botanists, after all, with a scientific mission and a mindset of gradual, rather than immediate, discovery. Decades later, in 1935, an American magazine quietly ran a tourism advertisement titled "More Curious Facts About Southern California," highlighting the counterintuitive discovery. Chief among these facts was a note that read: "First discovery of California gold was made *in England* in 1831. (Found on the roots of trees sent back by a Scottish botanist.)"

Douglas and Menzies saw value in the great trees that grew along the coast not solely as a resource or commodity or product, but in the details of their seeds and bracts, in the specific formation of their needles and the varying textures of their bark. But by the middle of the nineteenth century, eyes had begun to fall on

Vancouver Island's trees in earnest. Once again, the search for gold led the initial exploratory push. "So exciting is gold hunting that men are willing to leave the certainty of good wages to take the uncertainty of poor ones, led away by the hopes of striking large ones," wrote botanist and explorer Robert Brown in an 1864 resource survey of the island. In the Nitinat Valley, one of the largest watersheds on the west coast of the island, just up the coast from Port Renfrew, he remarked how the terrain was rough but the vast quantity and quality of forest he encountered held standing wealth beyond the uncertainty of a gold rush.

"The timber was however of the most magnificent description," Brown wrote. "Spars of Douglas pine and hemlock 100 to 150 feet in height & even higher, & from 2 to 3 feet in diameter, without a twig for 80 to 100 feet were shady in every direction, and the difficulty would not be in getting good ones, but in selecting among so many magnificent sticks... The timber alone would be a certain fortune."

Interest was budding, but the vast tracts of big timber had yet to be commercially exploited on a great scale. Trees larger than colonists had ever seen were useless without a method of extraction. What was principally needed was a means of transporting logs from the remote valleys and mountainsides to the coast, where they could be processed at mills or loaded onto ships. The job of constructing and maintaining the island's railroad fell to the Esquimalt & Nanaimo Railway Company. As compensation for the task, in 1884 the province of British Columbia handed over more than 750,000 hectares of land to the company, which began constructing lines and trestles into the heart of the island. Empty railcars went in and returned laden with logs. At thirteen years since the British colony became the sixth province of Canada, British Columbia was beginning to realize the magnitude of wealth that could be exploited in its forests.

Beginning in 1905, the province began selling timber licences (TLs)—one square mile of forest for ten dollars apiece—to prospectors or "cruisers." These leases allowed holders to cut, process, and sell any timber harvested off their TL, but once the trees were gone, the land would revert back to the province. Over the next century, this relationship has remained virtually the same: approximately 95 percent of British Columbia is publicly owned or Crown land, with leases granted to companies or individuals through a tenure agreement managed by the provincial government.

A Victoria-based timber operator named H. H. Jones wrote in *British Columbia Magazine*: "It was in 1906, when the timber fever was at its height! Cruisers, many of them of the tenderfoot order, were everywhere staking land, rock or water—anything that could be placed on paper, for the buyers were mostly of the same class as the cruisers: taking everything in sight, or, rather, out of sight, so long as it was called timber."

Even as early as 1912 there was concern over the rate of harvest, marked by British Columbia's minister of lands, William Roderick Ross, advocating for the passing of the Forest Act on the floor of the provincial legislature:

> An epoch, sir, is drawing to a close—the epoch of reckless devastation of the natural resources with which we, the people of this fair young Province, have been endowed by Providence—those magnificent resources of which the members of this Government and this Assembly are but the temporary trustees. That rugged rudimentary phase of pioneer activity is doomed to end. The writing is on the wall; the writing—to put the simple fact—is in this Forest Bill. Armed with that weapon, as forged by this honourable Assembly, the Government of British Columbia will undertake the work: of forest conservation.

The Forest Act appeared to signal an end to the Wild West of timber cruising in British Columbia, an era of "cut and get out." Ross spoke of "a past epoch condemned" and "a new epoch inaugurated" in terms of how British Columbians were going to see and value their forest lands.

"We glance down the vista of the years to come, and, turning from that vision of the future, we call the world to witness that we legislate today," the minister concluded, "not only for ourselves and for the needs of this day and this generation, but also, and no less, for our children's children, and for all posterity—that we may hand down to them their vast heritage of forest wealth, unexhausted and unimpaired."

While Ross spoke of conservation, he was actually more concerned with economics—with reinventing a forestry system that had led to a commercial shortfall for the provincial government, and therefore the public, for years.

To spur economic growth, the Forest Act attached strict requirements on the timber company holding a licence. "All timber cut on Crown lands... shall be used in this Province or be manufactured in this Province into boards, deal, joints, lath, shingles, or other sawn lumber," the original 1912 Forest Act stated, noting a few exceptions such as telephone poles. What were known as "appurtenancy clauses" required some licence holders to invest not just in the mechanisms for resource extraction but in communities themselves. Timber companies were required to saw or pulp their logs at mills within the very area that was being logged. A tree cut in the town of Lake Cowichan would have to be milled in Lake Cowichan. These rules led to a decades-long employment boom across Vancouver Island, turning backwater communities into thriving timber towns. Throughout the 1970s, Port Alberni had one of the highest per-capita incomes of any community in British Columbia—based primarily on the region's valley-bottom big timber.

To manage the resource and develop its extraction and processing, the provincial government created an institution alongside the 1912 Forest Act, the Forest Service. It also began collecting "stumpage fees"—a form of tax paid by timber companies to the government. Initially determined by the number of trees cut, "per stump," the fee became based on the volume of timber cut off a company's leases, measured in cubic metres or board feet. By measuring a tree's circumference with a tape and its height with a hypsometer, forest engineers could estimate the volume of wood held within to assess the total value of a stand. Stumpage fees created economic incentives for the government to support its timber industry, even when cries of concern arose over both the depletion of a resource as well as degradation of the environment.

In 1918, the Commission of Conservation in British Columbia published a report of the province's forest inventory. Even then, the commission recognized a dire state: "When one considers that the total stand of saws material in the whole Dominion probably does not greatly exceed this amount now, the seriousness of this loss, which can be attributed very largely to public carelessness, becomes apparent." But this "loss" in question was not because of logging but from fire, and it highlights the foundational principle for Canadian forestry at the beginning of the twentieth century: cut it before it burns. Forest fire was an unpredictable force but a known entity. It would return, to some degree, each hot summer—devouring what was becoming the province's most valuable resource.

To lead the Forest Service, the government appointed as its first chief forester Harvey Reginald (or "H. R.") MacMillan. The Ontarian would go on to become one of the pioneers of private timber companies in British Columbia with the establishment of H. R. MacMillan Export Company Ltd.—a precursor to MacMillan Bloedel, one of the foremost timber companies working up and down the coast from 1951 to when it was sold in 1999. But in 1912, MacMillan began his career on the political side of timber with a report to the provincial legislature encouraging further and urgent development of the industry:

> The annual growth of the forests of British Columbia is even now, before they are either adequately protected from fire or from waste,

> certainly not less than five times the present annual lumber cut... It is not merely advisable to encourage the growth of our lumber industry until it equals the production of our forests—it is our clear duty to do so, in order that timber which otherwise will soon rot on the ground may furnish the basis for industry, for reasonable profits to operator and Government, for home-building and, in the last analysis, for the growth of British Columbia.

This "clear duty," as MacMillan called it, framed much of British Columbia's perspective towards logging through the twentieth century—that it was the province's obligation to cut and use its primary resource before it was too late.

The end of the First World War saw a rapid expansion of timber harvesting on Vancouver Island and across the province. During the first four decades of the twentieth century, whoever held leases on land could cut whatever was desired at a rate regulated entirely by what they could sell. As long as a licence had been granted by the provincial government, nearly any tree, or any amount of trees, was up for grabs. What held the period in relative check wasn't forethought or restraint or resource management, but technology. Logs were not nuggets of gold that could be transported with ease.

The process of felling a tree and moving a log to mill was a tedious and tiresome act.

CUTTING A TREE BEGAN as an intimate task: one man and an axe. While pairs or teams often worked to take down a large tree, every swing and blow of the axe was felt and every chunk removed was hard-earned. But throughout the twentieth century, technological evolution and development in machinery refined the process of felling a tree from a plodding chore to a swift act. Photographs of loggers of the late 1800s and early 1900s, first with axes and then with crosscut handsaws, depict men balancing on springboards—planks of wood wedged into notches carved into a tree's trunk as high as three metres off the ground—slowly chipping away or gradually cutting into a behemoth fir or cedar or spruce. When the tree came down, it would have been the culmination of days of work—marked by a soft crack as the trunk finally gave way, a silence as the tree floated weightless for a moment, and an earth-shattering boom as the log struck the ground.

The 1970s saw the development of feller bunchers—backhoe-like vehicles with extendable saw arms capable of chopping, de-limbing, and cutting trees to length. These efficient machines cut forest like a combine harvester cuts wheat, and made it possible for loggers to clear an entire hectare of trees on level ground within a day. But in the Pacific temperate old-growth forests of coastal British Columbia, there is no machine capable of felling trees on such uneven ground. And more simply, the trees are just too big. Every great tree growing on Vancouver Island is brought down by hand—by a logger standing beside a colossal trunk with a saw.

Over the course of the twentieth century, the felling of a tree changed dramatically. In 1905, Samuel J. Bens of San Francisco, California, began experiments with mechanizing the laborious task of felling a tree by crosscut saw. His goal was to create a machine—an "endless chain saw"—capable of taking down his state's giant redwoods. Over the next two decades, various versions of a gasoline-powered small-engine saw with a sharp-toothed chain were tested. One, developed in 1918, weighed 210 pounds and was mounted on a 4.5-by-6-foot frame. Still, it wouldn't be until after the Second World War that anything resembling a modern chainsaw began to appear on the Canadian market, and by 1960 it still weighed more than twice a twenty-first-century model. Each development in technology allowed for more timber to be more effectively harvested—turning what might have taken a full day's work into a task accomplished in mere minutes. While it could take five hundred years for a tree to reach fifty metres in height and two metres in width, it could take five minutes for a skilled faller with a chainsaw to bring it down.

Felling big timber is an act similar to hunting big game. There is a quest to locate the prime of the species; there is a gradual approach towards a calm moment when the trigger is pulled; and there is a rumble and crashing to earth when the great beast is bagged. Except, on the open savannah, an elephant or a rhino can flee from hunters, possibly even fight back. In timber there is no chase—just a search and a kill.

The men who stalked the forests of British Columbia in search of big timber weren't the legendary lumberjacks of eastern Canadian folklore, magnanimous in iconic plaid shirts while running logs down the river. The lumbermen of the west were *fallers*—who lived and breathed the bush, without glamour or glory. They were rough-and-tumble men of work who burned their years with hands perennially coated in pitch, hair smelling of cedar, and burned their earnings on whiskey and sex in the saloons of Vancouver and Victoria. Companies capitalized on this machismo. In the 1970s, one of the largest chainsaw manufactures, Stihl, produced an advertisement featuring hard-hatted fallers standing on an enormous cedar stump while cutting into another tree. The tagline read: "We Came. We Saw. We Conquered."

Despite the technological limitations of the early twentieth century, by 1920 British Columbia was producing half of all timber around the country, surpassing production in every other province. Locating the towering stands of timber took great effort, and felling trees was laborious; but the greatest challenge was engineering a way to move a log weighing thousands of kilograms out of the forest. At every level, working in timber has been one of the most dangerous jobs, with forestry still holding the highest percentage of work-related deaths from injury than any other sector in British Columbia.

One of the first jobs for someone entering the industry has been a chokerman, someone whose responsibility was to set (or "choke") cables around logs so that they could be pulled out of the forest. In charge of a team of "chokers" was a hooktender who oversaw the crew working the lines. Communication between workers was done by a series of commands shouted over hundreds of metres through the forest. Logs would be rigged up with cables and hauled by horse trains to a centralized collecting point and then loaded onto railcars. Because of the rough terrain and roads often strewn with slash, horses wore shoes studded with hobnails, just like a logger's caulk boots.

In 1897, the first steam-powered engine—called a "donkey engine"—was introduced to West Coast logging, replacing the animal trains as the primary means of hauling logs. It was more reliable, efficient, and didn't need to be fed. A simple engine that turned a spool to recoil a cable, the donkey engine transformed the ease with which logs were acquired from previously inaccessible locations. But if a log became stuck or pinched among the rough terrain, disaster could strike when it finally broke free and the tension in the cables propelled the log like a multi-tonne bullet through the forest.

To alleviate this danger, timber crews looked to the trees themselves. Sometimes, crews employed the strength and stability of large standing trees to help haul logs from a cutblock, by wrapping a cable around the trunk to use it as an anchor or yarding point. Standing trees used in logging operations needed to be sound and secure, healthy, and large enough to withstand the stress.

The most dangerous, and thus highest-paid, position was that of a high rigger. Using specialized boots with metal spurs attached at the inner ankle, and a loop of cord around the trunk, a high rigger would ascend a selected tall tree. With a hand axe and single-person cross-saw, the rigger would denude the tree of branches and chop off its top to create a freestanding pole—a "spar"—that was secured to the earth by its own natural root system and stabilized through a set of guylines. A series of cables and pulleys were rigged to the spar, allowing logs to be lifted into the air. This "high lead" system was much more stable and controlled than dragging a log along the ground, and removed any danger of one becoming caught on debris or rough terrain. Increased mechanization brought heavy machinery, namely the yarding tower, in which up to four cables could haul logs simultaneously to an extraction point.

At times the process of felling timber can appear clumsy, with trees tumbling this way and that, one on top of another, to the ground. At times it can appear indiscriminate, as if a bulldozer and wrecking ball would suffice. But there is a method, in which minuscule adjustments can be employed by the faller so that a tree lands exactly where intended. At other times the network of cables and pulleys extracting logs from the base of a mountain slope to a road appear as if part of a high-wire act in a big top tent. Cables can span a valley, known as "skylines," where logs are attached to dangling cables off a mainline and gradually removed from the cutblock that can be hundreds of metres away. It is a delicate process, from felling to extraction, where mistakes at any stage in the operation could lead to death or maiming. Fallers need to be cautious of dead treetops or limbs—known in the industry as "widowmakers"—that could break off and plummet earthwards. For choker crews, in attaching and managing cables there are risks of logs twisting or rolling, of one becoming loose and tumbling free.

Alongside the twentieth century's technological evolutions of how trees were felled and collected were developments in transportation—how to move a log from a deep valley at the heart of Vancouver Island to the mills on the coast. Even before the modern chainsaw revolutionized the industry, felling a tree was a straightforward task. But a fallen log in the middle of a forest is of no use to any timber company.

Along the coasts of Vancouver Island, companies would seek out stands growing on hillsides where the trees, once felled, would tumble down by their own great momentum into the ocean. They would then be rafted together into large booms and maneuvered around the island to the mainland mills. But the process was a delicate one: at any moment the log could be set loose, and in a flash begin its violent slide. A logger would have to keep an eye out for an unexpected shift, and deftly leap to safety or else be caught by a passing branch. When a log is loose, it "runs" down the hillside with such power and such force it can shatter another large tree if hit head-on or plough through smaller trees, creating a wake of destruction similar to a jetliner crash-landing in the forest.

Groves deeper in the interior of the island were accessed by railcar. The area around Shawnigan Lake, just outside Victoria, holds one of the most spectacular remnants of twentieth-century logging engineering anywhere in the world. In 1920, Canadian National Railways completed the longest wooden railway trestle not just anywhere in the country but in the entire Commonwealth, at 188 metres. It was also one of the tallest in the world, built 44 metres above the river. The Kinsol Trestle saw millions of logs of some of Vancouver Island's finest old growth shipped by railcar across its breadth, until it started to fall from use in the 1950s. Following the Second World War, many deactivated military trucks were sold cheaply to timber companies, converted to logging trucks that soon replaced the railcar as the primary means of transporting logs. This flexibility allowed companies to access groves that were previously unreachable. As the forests of the eastern half of Vancouver Island began to dwindle, and with new technology and methods of harvesting, timber companies began to slowly expand into the lush rainforests of the western edge, where some of the province's biggest and most valuable timber was found.

Increased mechanization in felling, and a transition away from more cumbersome means of transportation, turned British Columbia's timber industry into a commercial harvest that was the driving force of the province's economy. At the industry's pinnacle in 1966, B.C. produced nearly three-quarters of all sawn lumber in Canada. Despite ups and downs over the subsequent decades, by the end of the twentieth century, forest products accounted for 30 percent of all British Columbia's exports, the industry was producing more than $10 billion in total revenue, and one out of every ten jobs in the province was related to timber. Every old-growth cedar, spruce, and fir was vital to the industry, but each ancient tree's value extended well beyond what could be felled, milled, and sold—into the ground below and the air above.

AT FIRST GLANCE, the old-growth forests of Vancouver Island seem defined by life: deer and elk browsing on the tender tips of forest grasses, red-and-white spotted mushrooms erupting from the earth, and towering trees trembling in the wind. But it is death that makes these forests complex. "The woods are full of dead and dying trees, yet needed for their beauty to complete the beauty of the living... How beautiful is all Death!" wrote John Muir in his journals. That is the positive death of the coastal old-growth forests of British Columbia, the kind that feeds the next round of inhabitants, both floral and faunal. The churning in these forests is nearly imperceptible. It would take years of patient study to notice the movement. But it is there—turning and folding and regenerating without respite. While some of the giant trees live for many centuries, even a millennium, they will fall. And when a structure as tall as an apartment building comes down, shattered by lightning or forced over in a gale, it crashes to the forest floor with thunderous applause—for the metre-tall saplings growing in the dappled shadow welcome the sunlight that beams through the new gap in the canopy.

Every tree that falls naturally in an old-growth forest remains. Their hulking corpses sometimes break and shatter, while others hold nearly intact from root to tip. Instantly, after a fall, the moment the forest returns to silence, that log becomes a feeding ground for the pileated woodpecker and the red-tailed chipmunk, and home to the black bear and the marten. It also becomes a "nurse log"—a rotting tree that offers its tonnes of nutrients to opportunistic seedlings. A common sight in an old-growth forest is a dead cedar with hundred-plus-year-old hemlock trees with roots growing out of and hugging the log, the cedar's natural preservative—an anti-fungal and anti-bacterial chemical called thujaplicin—keeping the log nearly entirely intact for more than a century. Each natural death begets life. But these forests also play host to another kind of mortality. Unlike those trees that tumble naturally and become part of the biomass, those felled by human hands are hauled away. Not only is the life lost, but so is the life-giving death.

Since the early days of logging in British Columbia,

one sentiment has been common in the timber industry: that old-growth forests are "decadent" and have a shelf life with an expiry date. If not redeemed, the value of the forests will be lost. By the middle of the twentieth century, this perspective became firmly entrenched as the principal perspective of timber companies. In 1949, a classification system was proposed to determine "cull factors" for older trees. Features including broken tops, swollen knots, burls, and trunk cracks were used as examples that a tree was rapidly losing its value.

The governing ideology was that old-growth forests were diseased and dying ecosystems that needed to be converted into fresh, lively, and vibrant new stands through harvesting and replanting. While words like "decadent" and "over-mature" eventually faded from common use, in practice the perspective remains.

That argument has often been presented by members of the logging community—that the big, old trees are not as ecologically valuable as younger ones. On the surface, new seedlings planted in a clear-cut appear to grow more voraciously than the grandparents that once stood in their place. However, these surface-level conclusions are based on little more than casual observations, as opposed to scientific fact.

Through the latter half of the twentieth century, scientists began looking closely at the ecological mechanisms and forces at play in these old-growth forests, making discoveries that would eventually redefine how we understand the ecosystems. In a global study of 403 temperate and tropical tree species, including plots of Douglas fir, Sitka spruce, western red cedar, and western hemlock planted as early as the 1930s, researchers found tree growth to accelerate with age, rather than slow down, in 97 percent of the species examined—busting the myth that ancient trees are ecologically decadent. This rapid growth means that the oldest trees sequester an increasing amount of carbon with every passing year, becoming more and more important as sentinels against climate change. Replanted, second-growth forests, therefore, cannot match the productivity and ecological value of an unmanaged forest.

Even on a miniature scale these big trees play a crucial role. Researchers uncovered species of plant and insect that are endemic to the forest canopies of old-growth trees, living only in suspended soil on tree branches hundreds of feet above the ground. From moss on the forest floor to the tip of the tallest tree, this layer teems with obvious life. And here also lies the value: timber, pulp, and fibre for the loggers; or trees and forests that could be protected for environmentalists. But underground—supporting this layer of giants—is a structure as complicated, vast, and crucial as anything sprouting or frolicking above ground.

In 1997, a professor of forest ecology at the University of British Columbia named Suzanne Simard published a study that popularized a radical notion of the depth of ecological relationships in forests. What started as a chance observation ended up revealing a profound interconnectivity between trees. It began when she was a child, on holiday in British Columbia's interior rainforests, when her family dog, Jiggs, fell into an outhouse. A messy rescue ensued, with members of the family putting mattock and shovel to earth in a mad dash to free their beloved beagle. As the pile of dirt grew, Simard's attention turned to the multicoloured layers of excavation and the dense mass of tree roots. Jiggs was eventually freed, but Simard focused on a filigree of white strands running through the soil. The strands—a kind of fungi—were about the diameter of a human hair and exceptionally fragile. The moment of panic had turned to inspiration for Simard, who went on to complete a degree in forestry at the University of British Columbia and would eventually teach and work in silviculture across the province—in a job assessing the successes and failures of reforestation after logging.

Simard's fascination with root networks led to work at the university, studying the relationship between fungi and trees. Fungi were once considered parasitic to a tree, but experiments by Simard and her team demonstrated a complex symbiotic relationship, called mycorrhiza. While the term had been coined in 1885—from the Greek *mykós* for "fungus" and *rhiza* for "root"—and associations between fungi and trees had been documented, it wasn't until the mid-1990s that the depth of this relationship began to be realized.

In an experiment, Simard and her colleagues set out to map these mycorrhizal networks. In the relationship between fungus and tree, thin strands of mycorrhizal fungi attach on a tree's roots and spread throughout the forest to connect with other fungi that have colonized other trees. After injecting a tree with a harmless radioactive isotope, they were able to trace the isotope using a Geiger counter, as the tree photosynthesized carbon dioxide into sugars. As the sugars descended the tree's trunk, so too did the isotope—into the ground, into the network of mycorrhizal fungi, and up into neighbouring trees. The strands of fungi were in fact tubes of a superhighway tunnel system, a massive underground network that connected trees together.

Both organisms benefit from this relationship: the trees provide much-needed sugars to the fungi, and the fungi absorb nutrients, including nitrogen and phosphorus, from the soil that they provide to the trees. Nitrogen, in particular, is a key building block for trees to grow big; without the mycorrhizal fungi, the trees of the Pacific temperate rainforests of Vancouver Island would never achieve such great heights.

The interconnectivity extends throughout the entire forest column, below ground and above, best illustrated in the relationship between the region's top three natural icons: trees, bears, and salmon. Along the coast, streams and rivers connect the Pacific Ocean to their mountain sources and provide the breeding grounds for salmon to lay their eggs. Old-growth forests that fringe these rivers and estuaries are key to a successful salmon run, by stabilizing the banks with their root networks and filtering meltwater that trickles down from the mountains or rainwater that falls throughout the forest. With healthy salmon populations come healthy bear populations. But when the salmon are plentiful—leaping in great numbers against the current to reach the cool, calm pools in which they lay their eggs—the bears become selective. It is common to see a bear catch a fish in its mouth, carry it ashore, and feed only on the richest and fattiest part: its brain. After a feed, corpses of headless salmon lie scattered along riverbanks and become a source of food for scavengers such as ravens and crows. But the protein-rich flesh also decomposes into the soil. Typically, the nutrient injection of the salmon's natural death cycle benefits plant growth within a thin riparian zone around a river, but bears have been seen carrying fish nearly a kilometre into the forest—as if they were gardeners dumping fertilizer directly onto the bases of trees. And because salmon can travel rivers to return to spawning grounds up to a thousand kilometres inland, this relationship can penetrate far from the immediate coastline.

Scientists could not only imagine a benefit to tree growth, but were also able to document a particular nitrogen molecule found in salmon within the very rings of the trees themselves. As the salmon decomposed, the mycorrhizal fungi absorbed the nitrogen and fed it to the trees. Not only did this process provide a historical record of which years were a salmon boom, for example, but it also revealed a measurable and profound connection between three key features of coastal forests: the bears eat the salmon; the decomposing carcasses of the salmon feed the trees; and the trees stabilize the habitat for the salmon and provide homes for the bears. At the pinnacle of this triangle are the large Sitka spruce, western red cedar, and Douglas fir.

The level of connection extends beyond resource-sharing. In times of drought or seasonal change, trees can use their mycorrhizal network as a storehouse for sugars accumulated during growth seasons, until they are needed. The networks have also been found to be used for a kind of arboreal 911 call between trees. When a tree is attacked by an insect, it can send a chemical signal through the mycorrhizal network to its neighbours, triggering them to release a defence mechanism such as a volatile organic compound that is harmful to the insect.

The concept of a whole ecosystem with organisms dependent on one another was not new, but research by scientists such as Suzanne Simard helped change how forests had previously been seen: as clusters of trees growing independently and even competing for resources, space, and light. There is less a life-or-death race to the top than a collaborative effort for success.

What became clear was that the largest trees were the nuclei of this network—drawing nutrients from their great height to sustain those growing in the shadows below. Over time, Simard discovered that the largest and oldest trees in the forest contained the most expansive networks of mycorrhizal connections. She found one Douglas fir to be linked with forty-seven other trees in its neighbourhood.

"Although trees from all cohorts were linked, large mature trees acted as hubs with a higher degree of connectivity," Simard and her colleagues wrote in their cleverly titled follow-up study "Architecture of the wood-wide web" in 2009. The largest mature trees had the most-developed root systems and therefore the deepest networks, and "they accounted for most of the connectivity and centrality among nodes in the network."

Also critical to the optimal functionality of this

network is a range of ages among the trees. A replanted, second-growth forest composed of single-age trees does not benefit as much as one with a spectrum of generations.

When an old-growth forest is clear-cut, more than the trees disappear. Without the trees providing sugars, the mycorrhizal fungi die—and it can take years, if not decades, after a cutblock is replanted for the underground network to re-form. Over time, fungi may eventually creep in from neighbouring forests, but the young seedlings are on their own in more ways than on the surface. They are tasked with not only regrowing into a forest, but also helping to re-establish a subterranean network critical to the health and sustainability of the broader ecosystem.

Simard's 2009 study concludes: "To ensure that old-growth Douglas fir forests remain resilient and self-regenerative following disturbance, our findings support a management approach that conserves large trees or groups of trees and their mycorrhizal fungal associates."

When left standing, the oldest and largest trees of these coastal forests play perhaps the most critical role: as the stewards of the forests, they ensure the viability of the forest, both in the present and in the future. The argument to protect the largest trees isn't purely a sentimental one. They aren't simply the last of their kind or an example of a species that we will never see again if completely harvested—these big trees are vital to the stability of our coastal forest ecosystems. Their vast networks of roots bind the landscape together and offer the foundation on which every kind of smaller life—mammals, fish, insects, other trees—can thrive.

In 1954, the British Columbia Ministry of Forests inventoried Vancouver Island's forests and produced a map of the existing supply. Its assessment placed the number of hectares of old-growth forest—those untouched by commercial logging—at 1.69 million, or approximately half of the island's total area. Over the following four decades, 24,000 hectares of the island's old-growth forests were cut annually—an amount equal to sixty Stanley Parks, Vancouver's iconic urban green space. By 1990, there was only 829,000 hectares of old-growth forest; more than half had been logged. And in the southern half of the island, where the hub of the region's timber history had buzzed for a century, it was estimated that only 25 percent of the original forests that had been standing in 1954 remained.

In the early 1990s, environmental groups were estimating that if the annual cut continued at the rate and volume it had maintained over the preceding four decades, Vancouver Island's unprotected old growth would be eliminated by 2022. All that would remain would be the few patches in provincial parks and recreation sites.

The rest would be replanted clear-cuts in various stages of regrowth. Between 1990 and 2015, the island saw its remaining old-growth forests decline by approximately 30 percent. By comparison, the Food and Agriculture Organization of the United Nations found that over the same twenty-five-year period, primary forests—those that are "globally irreplaceable with unique qualities that make significant contributions to biodiversity conservation, climate change mitigation, and sustainable livelihoods"—located in tropical countries declined by only 10 percent. While deforestation in Latin America and Southeast Asia often attracts attention, the forests of Vancouver Island are disappearing at a faster rate. In 2016, the British Columbia chapter of the Sierra Club, the U.S.–based environmental advocacy organization founded in 1892 by John Muir, announced Vancouver Island's old growth was in a "state of ecological emergency." Catastrophic ecological damage, including species loss, was imminent if the timber industry was left unchecked.

The Sierra Club B.C. subsequently released a map of the island's remaining old-growth stands, calling them "as rare as white rhinos." In the island's highly productive valleys, decades of commercial logging had reduced this specific slice of old growth—where the oldest, largest, and consequently rarest trees grow—to less than 7 percent of what originally stood. What had occurred was a century of furious harvesting on the island, fed by an overarching notion that these trees will never be extinguished and this seemingly inexhaustible resource will never be depleted.

To sail along the serrated west coast of the island, watching the wall of grand trees that buffer the storms pass by, is to be misled. These are among Vancouver Island's finest forests, but they are little more than a mirage—a thin fringe of lush, complex rainforest that obscures a harsh reality. Behind that wall of green gold lies the truth of Vancouver Island's forest legacy.

CHAPTER 5

War for the Woods

IN 1945, A COMMISSION was held to assess the future of British Columbia's forestry industry. The Sloan Commission, named after provincial chief justice Gordon Sloan, brought one issue into focus: the management and sustainability of harvesting the highest-value timber reserves, the old-growth forests.

Sloan's report marked the first earnest push to change forest policy in British Columbia: "At present our forest resources might be visualized as a slowly descending spiral," it read. "That picture must be changed to an ascending spiral. Differently phrased, we must change over from the present system of unmanaged and unregulated liquidation of our forested areas to a planned and regulated policy of forest management, leading eventually to a programme ensuring a sustained yield from all our productive land area." The consensus was that forests must be seen "as the source of renewable crops and not as a mine"—in other words, a resource that can be managed and replenished rather than drained.

Based on Sloan's recommendations, the Forest Act was amended in 1947 to create a form of tenure known as tree farm licences (TFLS), large blocks of Crown land leased to timber companies on a long-term, renewable basis. These blocks are broken up into individual cutblocks of one or two dozen hectares. TFL 33 surrounds Kamloops in the province's interior. TFL 39 encompasses much of the northern half of Haida Gwaii. And TFL 46 runs north of Port Renfrew and includes some of the most productive valleys on Vancouver Island. To manage the rate of harvest, the Sloan Commission suggested that the province's forest harvesting be regulated by an allowable annual cut (AAC)—a maximum volume of timber that can be extracted in a given year, as set by the chief forester. The AAC was meant to serve as a regulatory measure to limit the amount of trees that could be cut by timber companies to avoid overharvesting, but still allowed for controversial techniques, including clear-cutting.

The focus of the commission was more on managing and re-establishing the resource than any kind of environmental degradation. Out of fear that the harvest was unsustainable long term, Sloan recommended an increase in the rate of tree planting, as well as a greater diversity of species planted. Of the seven million seedlings that were planted in 1955, the vast majority were Douglas fir that companies had been casually planting after cutting, as a means to ensure future supply. Sloan's objective of 38.4 million seedlings planted annually was never met, and it wasn't until 1987 that timber companies were required by law to replant their cutblocks.

Sloan's objective was for planted second growth to eventually replace the original old growth so that, as the latter decreases, the former is supplanting the timber supply. But there was concern that by the time all the old growth was cut, the second growth wouldn't be ready, and this gap would lead to a "fall down" effect—a social and economic collapse.

With burgeoning economic tensions coupled with a rise in North American environmentalism (precipitated in 1962 by the publication of American biologist Rachel Carson's *Silent Spring*), alongside the furious pace of resource extraction on Vancouver Island came a more gradual rise in anti-logging activism. Environmentalists—often starting out as recreational hikers—began to delve deeper along logging roads and came to realize the extent to which the timber companies had cut away the forests.

Both activists and loggers were hunting for the same thing: the island's lush valley bottoms, where trees of the Pacific temperate rainforest not only grow well, they grow big. There stood great value for both parties. To the loggers, each great tree, if felled, represented tens of thousands of dollars in prized timber. And to the environmental activists, the groves, if left standing, could be turned into a park or recreation zone for tourists and hikers.

In the spring of 1988, environmental activist Randy Stoltmann went looking for Canada's tallest tree. Rumours had been swirling for years that a giant Sitka spruce had been identified in the 1950s in one of the major watersheds on the southern half of Vancouver Island—in the Carmanah Valley. Few places on the entire coast are quite as sublime an exemplar of Pacific temperate old-growth forest than that which grows along the banks of the Carmanah Creek. The valley is broad and flat, with rich silt banks, accumulated over centuries of flooding, that offer the ideal canvas to grow a forest.

"It was an incredibly inspiring place; a living cathedral. None of us had seen groves of trees that tall in B.C.," wrote Paul George in his history of the Western Canada Wilderness Committee (WCWC), an environmental education and activism organization he co-founded in 1980.

Legends of the giant tree date back to 1956, when Mike Gye, a twenty-nine-year-old timber surveyor for MacMillan Bloedel, was working in the lower reaches of the Carmanah Valley. Around two kilometres inland from the Pacific Ocean, where the West Coast Trail would eventually be formalized by the establishment of the Pacific Rim National Park Reserve in 1970, Gye stumbled upon an enormous tree. He measured the Sitka spruce a couple of times, concluding that the tree exceeded ninety metres in height. If confirmed, it would not only be the country's tallest tree but the tallest known Sitka spruce in the world.

Over the following decades, MacMillan Bloedel turned its attention away from the forests of Carmanah to those more easily accessed elsewhere on Vancouver Island. The record-breaking spruce wasn't even entered into the company's official inventory; in the mid-1950s there were still many trees of similar stature. Gye's spruce faded from story to myth: Canada's tallest tree was out there, somewhere within a dense forest spanning thousands of hectares, waiting to be found once again.

Based on everything Stoltmann knew about the geography and ecology of Carmanah, if the country's tallest tree would be growing anywhere, it would be there, in the wet trough of the valley. As a member of the WCWC and an avid big-tree hunter, Stoltmann had explored much of Vancouver Island's forests. And the spring of 1988 wasn't the first time he had gone looking for the legendary tree of Carmanah. Six years earlier he had been dropped by helicopter on one of the gravel bars along the creek. He'd hiked up and down the valley, and while he never located the record-breaker he did document some towering Sitka spruces. In his 1987 book *Hiking Guide to the Big Trees of Southwestern British Columbia*, he described how after only eight hours in the valley he was left stunned by what he had found, calling it "perhaps the finest remaining stand of virgin Sitka spruces in Canada." The size of the trees was remarkable, but so was the density of the grove: hundreds of Sitka spruces, with their column-straight trunks covered in scale-like bark, appeared at every turn through the lush undergrowth. Still, among pages of descriptions, directions, and hand-drawn maps dedicated to the great trees and forests of the island, Stoltmann only mentioned the forests around Carmanah Creek in an appendix. While tens of thousands of hikers walking the West Coast Trail crossed the creek as it spills into the Pacific Ocean along the coastline, few ventured inland. For decades, even timber companies had focused their operations elsewhere.

When Stoltmann returned for his second excursion into the valley, with fellow activist Clinton Webb, he noticed the great trees of Carmanah Valley were under imminent threat. Hundreds of hectares of forest around the valley had already been clear-cut, and a road had been constructed right to the edge—directly above the grove of huge Sitka spruces he had previously strolled through. And when he hiked down into the valley itself, he found flagging and spray paint on trees. To the activists it was clear: MacMillan Bloedel, the company that owned the tree farm licence for that area, was hoping to log the towering trees of Carmanah before anyone noticed.

AFTER STOLTMANN DISCOVERED THE logging road and flagging, he went to check on MacMillan Bloedel's five-year cutting plan. In December 1984, the company had received approval from the provincial Forest Service for their proposal, which included every region that the company intended to log within tree farm licence 44, a massive 450,000-hectare holding in southern Vancouver Island. There was no indication that Carmanah was part of that five-year plan. Stoltmann found out, however, that shortly after receiving approval following a public review period, MacMillan Bloedel had adjusted the boundaries of its plan. The company had made the modification with the consent of the provincial government, which agreed to approve logging in Carmanah as early as 1989. The move placed the lower portions of the valley—that "living cathedral," as Paul George would call it—under imminent danger of being cut. The *Vancouver Sun* ran an article shortly thereafter titled "Tree hunter's claim of forest giants sparks preservation plea," in which a MacMillan Bloedel spokesperson said that he "would be surprised if we can't find spruce of equal size already preserved," in an attempt to downplay the ecological significance and rarity of Carmanah's forests.

To the activists, it became clear not only that Carmanah would be a new battleground but that it could also could be turned into their flagship campaign. While it was less than a decade old, the Western Canada Wilderness Committee had already achieved success in activism campaigns focused on protecting biodiversity and wilderness areas. In the mid-1980s, protests led by the WCWC on South Moresby on Haida Gwaii, then known as the Queen Charlotte Islands, included dozens of arrests for violating an injunction against blocking logging roads, but ultimately led to the establishment of the South Moresby National Park Reserve.

In May 1988 in Carmanah, amid growing pressure, MacMillan Bloedel agreed to a month-long stalemate and to temporarily halt the construction of three logging roads around Carmanah. The decision was made to avoid confrontation with protestors, but also so the company could conduct a thorough assessment of the timber value in the valley. It wanted to know exactly how much money was at stake. The WCWC rushed to do the same—not to determine the monetary value but to gauge the potential usefulness to their cause. They wanted to find and measure as many giants as possible—the bigger the trees, the bigger the public outcry. The organization began by sending groups, spearheaded by Stoltmann, to build a trail into the valley. The protestors built two base camps. One, down near the river in the middle of the old growth, was known as Camp Heaven, and another, out of the valley alongside the muddy logging road in a clear-cut, was dubbed Camp Hell. While remnants or traces of each have long since been cleaned up or overgrown by the forest, the first is memorialized by one of the broadest Sitka spruces in the valley, known as Heaven Tree, with a base diameter of 3.5 metres and a height of 77 metres.

Quietly, both activists and timber workers were also looking for the fabled giant Sitka spruce. Since Mike Gye had stumbled upon the tree in 1956, it had only continued to grow. But in the spring of 1988, for both groups, Gye's fabled spruce became a Holy Grail. While the environmentalists were hiking the valley searching for big trees on foot, MacMillan Bloedel was buzzing above the canopy in a helicopter. From their aerial view, the magnitude of the grove of Sitka spruces became clear. It was a collection of such density, it rivalled the great groves of old that early twentieth-century loggers had put their axes to. After a reconnaissance flight, a MacMillan Bloedel forester remarked that just one of these spruces could fetch $40,000; but processed and sold as higher-market products to companies that build furniture or guitars, it could be worth double that. With each venture farther up and down the valley, more enormous trees were identified and recorded. They found them in dense groves that, if uprooted and planted in downtown Victoria, would be landmarks seen from anywhere the city.

Still, they hunted for the big one, the rumoured Sitka that would shatter records. One MacMillan Bloedel forester commented at the time: "We hope that these trees aren't the biggest or the tallest, so that we can just come in here and log them." But in early June, a MacMillan Bloedel helicopter circled over a portion of the Carmanah Valley just inland from where the creek trickles into the Pacific Ocean. The team located one tree with a delicate top well above the forest canopy, dropped a chain, and were stunned when it touched the ground: ninety-five metres. It was the tallest Sitka spruce in the world. They had found Gye's legendary tree.

It was members of the timber company who gave the tree a name—the Carmanah Giant—but it was activists who were most excited by the confirmation.

The tree, estimated to be between five hundred and seven hundred years old, became a rallying point for the entire anti-logging protest. Public attention intensified. Nearly every news article about the conflict included mention of the record-breaking tree. It was called the "king of the valley" and a "national treasure." It was a single tree that people could unite around and that petitions could be written about. It had a legendary story, a name, and a superlative. *How could we possibly cut down Canada's tallest tree?*

In the face of mounting pressure, MacMillan Bloedel needed to relieve the tension. "It's very unlikely it would be cut," Dennis Bendickson, a manager for the timber company, told the *Vancouver Sun* shortly after the Carmanah Giant had been found. "It's a significant tree and our policy always has been to protect trees like that." It was an admission that gave few assurances to activists watching trucks continue to haul logs out of the region's forests.

The Western Canada Wilderness Committee recognized the potential this one tree held as a symbol. "You have to make a poster of that tree and get it out right away," one member of the organization told Paul George. "It'll become the icon that saves the whole valley." The WCWC hired a helicopter for a photographer to shoot the tree and turn the image into a poster. George had high hopes, but admitted that when the photographer's images were developed he wasn't impressed—the tree looked like a "giant shrub." The tallest tree in Canada didn't look that tall nestled in a thick forest along a riverbank. George was hoping for awe, but was left underwhelmed. And even Randy Stoltmann, who was photographed at the tree's base to provide scale, didn't look as small as the organization was hoping for. The poster project cost the organization $4,000 and was never printed for public sale. Still, even without an evocative image, the story of the Carmanah Giant spread well beyond the confines of the valley—becoming a legendary beacon for visitors to the area. By the end of the summer, the trail from Camp Heaven to Canada's tallest tree would be completed.

UP UNTIL THE SUMMER OF 1988, timber companies across Vancouver Island had enjoyed near-unchecked reign. There had been minor protests, mere blips in their relentless harvest of big timber, but it wasn't until Carmanah Valley that the battle over the island's old-growth forests became a national and international issue. But pressure within the logging industry was also mounting. Mills were beginning to be closed around the island and timber workers were starting to feel a change in the air—one that with enough momentum could threaten their employment. Giving up even a few hundred hectares to environmental activists didn't just represent a concession; it represented the snowflake that could cause the avalanche. One tree didn't just represent several hundred cubic metres of timber; it represented a job.

In late June, MacMillan Bloedel put forward their first of several offers to placate the activists. The proposed nine-hectare protected zone around the Carmanah Giant and a ninety-hectare one in the valley—representing just 1.4 percent of the entire Carmanah watershed—was rejected by the Western Canada Wilderness Committee outright. In October, the timber company offered to increase the protected zone to 2 percent, and then in January 1989 to 7 percent. Both were dismissed by the environmental group as token offers that would allow the vast majority of the valley to be cut.

As the WCWC fought MacMillan Bloedel in the courts, activists doubled their efforts to begin turning Carmanah Valley into a park—in appearance if not in title. In part because people wanted to participate in the anti-logging protests, and in part to stand among the valley's legendary trees, visitors began flocking to Carmanah. To accommodate them, and lessen the environmental impact of hundreds of people traipsing through the forest, activists began formalizing the trail that connected Camps Heaven and Hell, activity that MacMillan Bloedel officials strenuously opposed.

Over the summer of 1988, volunteers continued to carve out trails to create a network leading to the most significant and largest trees. In August, protestors focused on blazing a path to the West Coast Trail, one of the most famous hiking trails in the country, as well as connecting Carmanah with Walbran Valley to the south. In one steep section of the ravine, they used a chainsaw to cut steps into a fallen cedar log to create a dramatic natural staircase into the valley.

Constructing path networks in proposed logging sites became an effective tactic of environmental groups. Activists recognized that if they could establish even informal recreation sites in Carmanah, Walbran, and elsewhere, hikers and campers frequenting the area would act as a deterrent to timber companies. Promoting a forest for its tourism potential, in a bid to establish a near-permanent presence of visitors, would in theory force a timber company to reassess their cutting plans. Or, more simply, it would establish a platform on which the value of a particular forest could be conveyed to the greatest number of people. But the activists knew the clock was ticking, and they opted not to wait for official government permission to build trails on Crown land, instead organizing numerous expeditions into Carmanah Valley to clear paths to many of the watershed's most spectacular features: trees, pools, waterfalls. After just one year in the news,

Carmanah was called "one of Canada's most popular wilderness destinations." Recognizing that with an influx of visitors would come greater public awareness of their logging plan to fell some of the country's largest trees, in response MacMillan Bloedel called the trail "dangerous to hike" in an attempt to discourage people from visiting.

On one expedition, a caravan of 150 WCWC trail builders, activists, and supporters ran into a locked gate, as well as a piece of heavy machinery and a pile of logs blocking the road several kilometres before the trailhead to the valley. Paul George saw it as an ideal opportunity: they had travelled with a camera crew, to gather footage for a documentary called *Carmanah Forever.* In the film, an activist presents George with a letter from MacMillan Bloedel, which he reads aloud: "Please be advised that persons engaged in unauthorized construction activity, including trail construction within the vicinity of Carmanah Creek, are to cease and desist immediately. These activities are unauthorized and therefore illegal under the current management working plan and under the current cutting permit for tree farm licence 44." The shot took several takes, but in the end was a perfectly choreographed moment that demonstrated the tension between the two groups and their fight for the valley. To host *Carmanah Forever,* the WCWC turned to David Suzuki, renowned environmental activist, author, and host of CBC's hit documentary series *The Nature of Things.* The iconic—and familiar—face and voice described scenes of dusty clear-cuts juxtaposed with those from the verdant valley bottom. Suzuki called the region "irreplaceable" and argued that "preserving a single tree or isolated grove will not ensure the forest's survival." The film was a success as a tool for activism as well as for education, being shown in classrooms across British Columbia.

But most people around the country, even many who lived in Victoria and Vancouver, had never stood beside a tree with a trunk wider than their vehicle or taller than their office building. Without standing under them, tracing a long gaze from root to tip, the size of the trees was hard to convey. The WCWC campaign in Carmanah needed to show people who would never make the journey, which included a three-hour drive on bumpy logging roads, the scale of these trees.

Paul George commissioned nature photographer Adrian Dorst to photograph Carmanah for a poster. "As luck would have it," George wrote in his history of the WCWC, "on the same day Adrian arrived to pick up the camera and film, a petite biology student from eastern Canada serendipitously walked into our office." She became the model, the point of scale that would demonstrate the size of Carmanah's behemoth trees. The result was a simple but evocative image that depicted a young woman dwarfed by a towering grove of trees. With the tagline "Carmanah: Big Trees not Big Stumps," the poster was a hit, reprinting many times and selling tens of thousands of copies.

Carmanah became a hotbed for biologists interested in studying the canopy ecosystems of Pacific temperate rainforests. To raise funds to build and maintain a research station in the treetops of a seventy-five-metre-tall Sitka spruce—in what would become the first research platform in the canopy of a temperate rainforest anywhere in the world—the WCWC began an adopt-a-tree campaign. Thousands around the country mailed in twenty-five dollars with a chosen name and received a certificate in return.

The main argument for protecting Carmanah was emotional, centring on the rarity of the trees and the rarity of the grove. It marked a spark of an internal confrontation within many Canadians, between what kind of country Canada has always been—rich through its resources—and what it was working to become: environmentally progressive. Carmanah epitomized this strife. Simply standing under its towering trees and looking up was to be forced to grapple with a country's dark past in resource extraction. It was to imagine two possible futures: one where Canadians will never again experience a feeling of awe at some of nature's biggest creations, and another where these rare trees are recognized for their enduring value and protected.

Over the summer of 1989, four expeditions made up of some of Canada's most renowned artists ventured into the Carmanah Valley. Acclaimed Canadian painters Robert Bateman, Jack Shadbolt, and Gordon Smith were among the approximately one hundred artists who camped along the riverbank to paint, photograph, and sketch. The artists focused on a variety of aspects of the Pacific temperate rainforest: the massive trees, the subtle details in the undergrowth, the scope of the forested hills, the contrast in a clear-cut.

In an interview at the time, Jack Shadbolt summarized the experience: "Standing with my back to this big tree that's behind here, how can I help but feel something of a tremendous grandeur of natural growth—that the world has a certain kind of meaning?... I like to live somewhere near that kind of feeling as an antidote to all the practical things I have to do in life just to survive."

Robert Bateman, known for his realistic paintings of animals and landscapes, found himself drawn to the clear-cuts—it was as if he were looking at piles of bones. The work he produced that summer depicted a grey and scattered cutblock above a panel of intact forest.

Artists had always been drawn to these forests, to capture the wilds of British Columbia. Chief among them was Emily Carr. Born in Victoria in 1871, Carr built a career on condensing the scale and depth of the province's expansive nature onto her canvases. Her paintings plunged viewers into the heart of the forest, revealing the untamed and impenetrable aspects of the natural world as being both ethereal and inviting. In the darkest places, she found light: a beam through a canopy, or a highlighted branch. Carr also documented the destruction of these forests. In her 1966 book, *Hundreds and Thousands*, she wrote:

> Yesterday I went into a great forest, I mean a portion of growth undisturbed for years and years. Way back, some great, grand trees had been felled, leaving their stumps with the ragged row of "screamers" in the centre, the last chords to break, chords in the tree's very heart. Growth had repaired all the damage and hidden the scars. There were second-growth trees, lusty and fine, tall-standing bracken and sword ferns, salal, rose and blackberry vines, useless trees that nobody cuts, trees ill-shaped and twisty that stood at the foot of those mighty arrow-straight monarchs long since chewed by steel teeth in the mighty mills, chewed into utility, nailed into houses, churches, telephone poles, all the "woodsyness" extracted, nothing remaining but wood.

In 1931, Emily Carr painted *Scorned as Timber, Beloved of the Sky*—an image of a single slender tree with a hat-like crown, standing in a clear-cut surrounded by stumps.

Before Carmanah, campaigns to save British Columbia's old-growth forests rarely extended beyond the borders of the province. In the summer of 1988, several dozen activists were arrested for blockading roads in Clayoquot Sound, a mountainous watershed and forested archipelago on the west coast of Vancouver Island near Tofino, and were sentenced to between three and forty-five days in jail. The pattern was repeated in numerous other skirmishes across coastal British Columbia, including the Lower Tsitika Valley in 1990 and the Slocan Valley in 1991. But Carmanah, in part because of the celebrity artists and high-profile activists like David Suzuki, made the issue international. Canadian singer Bryan Adams took a tour of the valley and held a benefit concert in support of the Western Canada Wilderness Committee's campaign. Companies offered support as well: Mountain Equipment Co-op, the outdoor retailer founded in Vancouver in 1971, gave the activist organization access to its mailing list to use for a newsletter campaign, only to receive numerous complaints from people who were gear consumers but not preservationists.

The original artwork produced during the summer of 1989 was auctioned off to raise money for the legal battles over protecting the Carmanah Valley, and was later turned into a book, *Carmanah: Artistic Visions of an Ancient Rainforest*. "Campfire conversations would often turn to the stark contrast between the haunting beauty of Carmanah's virgin forest and the slash-choked, burned and blackened clear-cuts that lie just outside the watershed," the WCWC wrote in their newsletter that autumn. "The artists spoke of how the distant growl of heavy logging equipment, carried by the wind from the next valley, affected them... a constant reminder as they sketched and painted, of why they were there."

IN THE FALL OF 1990, a group of loggers blockaded the entrance to the Carmanah Valley, stopping the activists from reaching their treetop research station for two days. When the loggers relented, the activists found the Western Canada Wilderness Committee's research tent near Camp Heaven had been burnt to the ground, boardwalks had been axed, and bridges had been toppled into the creek—damage the WCWC estimated at more than $30,000.

But the battle for British Columbia's trees was waged not only along the dusty logging roads or deep in the forests of Vancouver Island, but on the airwaves and in advertising that could offer greater reach. While activist organizations marketed the value of protecting these big trees, logging companies launched campaigns that extolled the virtues of bringing them down. In the 1970s, MacMillan Bloedel produced *The Incredible Forest*, a film that rhapsodized about British Columbia's timber industry.

"This is the age of a new breed of fallers, buckers, skinners, choker-setters, and he comes with an army of foresters, logging engineers, cruisers, tree markers, and other scientists—armed with barometers, binoculars, microscopes, surveying instruments, thermometers, and test tubes," reads the narrator over romantic scenes of a logger hiking through a forest and felling a large Sitka spruce with his chainsaw.

"Timber!" the man shouts as the tree falls into a clear-cut.

"These are the loggers of today," the narrator continues, "living with and caring for the forests of tomorrow."

In another film produced by MacMillan Bloedel, titled *The Managed Forest*, the narrator calmly reads: "Forest managers know that seeing a freshly logged site can be a distressing emotional experience. The site looks utterly devastated. But forest managers also know clear-cutting is not only ecologically sound but also the safest and most economical way of logging B.C.'s coastal forest."

The most significant investment in marketing timber came in the late 1980s, leading up to the eruption of the movements to protect Carmanah Valley and Clayoquot Sound. In fear of losing the public relations battle, the Council of Forest Industries in British Columbia invested $1.5 million in an advertising campaign called "Forests Forever." The commercials featured plaid-wearing timber workers strolling happily through the forest, and hard-hatted children holding Douglas fir seedlings, while the voiceover praised the industry's responsible forest management and care for the environment. One even included what appeared to be a stuffed deer and a fake eagle. Many of the public—not just environmental activists—weren't convinced. They saw the advertisements as simple greenwashing: timber companies attempting to glamorize their work and paint over its faults. Soon, it became apparent that the campaign had produced the opposite effect than intended: even less trust of the forestry industry. As public opinion was beginning to shift, advertisements were created to counter to the "Forests Forever" campaign, including one featuring an animated young sapling asking his "grandfather"—who appears to be an aged spruce—if he will grow up to be just as big and strong.

The old tree expresses doubt: "Unless something is done soon, big old trees like me will be nothing but a memory..."

"What would the forest be without old ones like you?" the little sapling asks.

"I think they call it a tree farm, son."

The tagline read: "A Tree Farm is Not a Forest."

The so-called subvertisement, however, never saw airtime after being rejected by networks; it had been produced by Kalle Lasn, who shortly thereafter, in 1989, co-founded the Vancouver-based social activist media company Adbusters, in part over conservation battles with B.C. timber companies.

In 1990, a consortium of timber companies hired the New York public relations firm Burson-Marsteller, which had represented Union Carbide six years prior, after the gas leak in Bhopal, India, that caused between two thousand and four thousand immediate deaths and tens of thousands of long-term health issues. The firm formalized the consortium into the B.C. Forest Alliance and began a widespread marketing campaign to re-establish the timber industry's dominant and proud allure of decades past—when communities were expanding, jobs were plentiful, and resource tensions were nonexistent—and to undercut the growing environmentalist wave. Millions of dollars were invested into advertisements in print and on TV.

On the ground, timber companies tried to break the image of the peace-loving activist by driving the narrative of the radicalized anarchist. Protestors were called "eco-terrorists" in Carmanah, and likened to "anti-abortion protesters" in Clayoquot. Some tactics employed in Carmanah, Clayoquot, and Walbran were simply an attempt to stop loggers from accessing the trees. "Tree sitting" involved protestors climbing into the branches and remaining there for days or weeks on end as a human shield. In Carmanah, a twenty-year-old protester had to be medically evacuated by helicopter after sustaining injuries to her back and leg from falling out of her treetop perch. But the tactic that caused furor among timber communities and companies was much more assertive. "Tree spiking" involved someone hammering iron spikes into the base of large trees. These spikes would likely be harmless to such an enormous tree, but could be fatal to a faller who might hit a four-inch bolt of metal with their chainsaw. If the machine's chain, moving at more than eighty-five kilometres per hour through a soft cedar trunk, were to impact a solid piece of metal, the violent kickback could potentially lead to the amputation of an arm of a faller, or even death. In September 1991, a MacMillan Bloedel faller in the Walbran Valley narrowly escaped disaster when his chainsaw hit one. "It's like planting landmines or leaving little time bombs around," MacMillan Bloedel forester Gord Eason told the *Vancouver Sun*.

While tree spiking was roundly denounced by less radical activists, the practice continued regardless. Accusations about who exactly was spiking trees were thrown across the protest lines: loggers accused the activists, while Syd Haskell, president of the Carmanah Forestry Society, was certain that the timber workers planted the spikes themselves in an effort to paint the environmentalists as sinister. "I'm alleging that someone sympathetic to timber-cutting in the Walbran did this in order to discredit our image," he told the *Vancouver Sun* in the fall of 1991. "If there are trees being spiked, I have no doubt where they are coming from."

In the spring of 1992, after eighty-five spikes were discovered embedded in trees in the Walbran Valley, Joe Foy, campaign director of the Western Canada Wilderness Committee, condemned the act, calling it "a form of terrorism" and offering a $1,000 reward for information that would lead to arrests. His denunciation of this form of protest raised the ire of more radical anti-logging activists. Weeks after Foy's statement, someone filled the locks of the WCWC's downtown Vancouver office with glue and attached a poster to the door that bore his face and flipped his $1,000 reward onto Foy himself. "Responsible environmentalists work for the Earth, not for the police," read the poster. "Which side are you on? Remove the bounty."

Foy was unmoved. "You learn the most important things in the sandbox of a playground," the activist told the *Vancouver Sun*. "You don't hurt people and you don't put people at risk. Tree spiking creates fear and unnecessary stress for forest workers and their families."

The early 1990s were a period of intense fervour over the future of Vancouver Island's forests, but they ultimately ended with thousands of hectares of old growth off limits to logging. In June 1990, the province tabled a bill to establish Carmanah Pacific Park, removing the entirety of the valley from MacMillan Bloedel's tree farm licence. Five years later, portions of the neighbouring Walbran Valley were incorporated, forming the 16,365-hectare Carmanah Walbran Provincial Park. But the timber companies didn't leave Carmanah and Walbran empty-handed. The government of British Columbia paid MacMillan Bloedel $83.75 million for income lost.

Today, the Carmanah Giant still stands, but the trail along Carmanah Creek to the tree quickly became overgrown once the activists had achieved their goal of protecting the valley. Ferns and brambles reclaimed the track. The tree is only accessible along a two-kilometre detour off the West Coast Trail, far enough that few hikers opt for the diversion as they trudge along the coast. No activists or loggers lurk around its trunk, no helicopters hover at its top—the tallest tree in Canada, the Sitka spruce of legend, grows quietly once again.

CARMANAH WAS THE SPARK for forest activism on Vancouver Island that reached full flame farther up the coast of Vancouver Island, near the world-renowned surfer town of Tofino. The logging of Clayoquot Sound, which had been spurring minor protests since the early 1980s, turned the battle for Vancouver Island's old-growth forests into what was called the War in the Woods. The head-to-head between activists and timber workers culminated in the summer of 1993, with two hundred litres of excrement being dumped near the Western Canada Wilderness Committee's staging site, and around 950 protesters being arrested and 850 convicted of defying a court injunction against blockading logging roads. The protests were one of the largest acts of civil disobedience in the country's history. Greenpeace pushed for a boycott of forest products from British Columbia to pressure the industry to back down. In one of its more international campaigns, the WCWC dug up a nearly four-hundred-year-old cedar stump, loaded it onto a flatbed trunk, named it Stumpy, and toured it from the B.C. legislature in Victoria across the country to Ottawa under the banner "Clayoquot Sound NOT Clearcut Sound." It was then loaded onto a ship and toured England and Germany. In 1995, Clayoquot Sound was protected by provincial order, and in 2000 it was designated a UNESCO biosphere reserve.

For years, Carmanah and Clayoquot remained in the memories of both activists and timber workers. To activists, these battlegrounds became legendary as examples of how a handful of plucky environmentalists can stand up to Big Timber, how a war can be fought and won. Not only were trees saved, but the actions forced the Ministry of Forests to re-examine its policies. The same year as the formation of Carmanah Walbran Provincial Park, the Forest Practices Code of British Columbia Act became law, establishing new regulations for logging companies, reforestation policies, road construction, and the treatment of wildlife habitats and watersheds.

In 1991, the Forest Resources Commission had released *The Future of Our Forests*, a report that made it clear that B.C.'s timber industry was approaching a cliff edge. Forestry practices were focused on short-term returns, without considering long-term consequences or how these forests might offer sources of value other than planks and pulp.

For the fallers, hauling crews, and truck drivers, Carmanah represented a dark scar on British Columbia's timber history—a significant concession to appease environmentalists, one that took available resources off the table and therefore affected jobs. After decades working in the industry on Vancouver Island, one timber worker summarized that time of tension: "Boy, we lost that war."

CHAPTER 6

A Forest Alliance

WHILE THE 1990S WAS a decade of feverish activity around Vancouver Island's forests, the 2000s saw a dip in attention. The pro-forest focus began to migrate north up the coast, towards the region known as the Great Bear Rainforest. There, the elusive and mysterious "spirit bear," a subspecies of black bear with white fur, became a symbol of the rarity of these forests and helped galvanize the public to protect the region.

At the same time, the logging industry began to make its move. In the early 2000s, some of the province's largest timber companies—including Weyerhaeuser (which had purchased MacMillan Bloedel), Interfor, TimberWest—promised that if the government agreed to certain changes in the Forest Practices Code of

British Columbia Act, they would invest a billion dollars in the industry by building mills and investing in the research and development of value-added products, including engineered timbers (beams made from lower-value wood glued together). In 2002, the provincial government made good on its promise with the most significant amendments to forestry regulations in half a century, with the reformation of the Forest Practices Code into the Forest and Range Practices Act. After a series of clarifications and amendments, the act came into effect in 2004 and heralded a period of deregulation for the province's forestry industry, where the onus was placed on the individual forester or forestry company to follow regulations. "It was like putting a fox in a chicken coop and saying 'only take one,'" as a long-time forest engineer put it. Despite these changes to the code, of the $1 billion pledged by the logging companies, only a small fraction of the promised investment has materialized.

The changes also removed the appurtenancy clauses, which required timber cut on Crown lands to be "used" and "manufactured" in the province, clauses that had been in place since 1947, when the last major amendments were made to the 1912 Forest Act. Companies that held a licence to cut in a specific region had been required to invest in the construction and maintenance of mills, forcing companies to invest heavily in communities. After 2004, timber companies were no longer required, or penalized for failing, to maintain their existing mills or upgrade and retool them to accommodate smaller second-growth logs, a necessary condition to moving away from old-growth logging. Between 1997 and 2001, twenty-seven mills had closed across the province; between 2001 and 2011, seventy more were shuttered. Thousands of jobs were lost. In 2001, TimberWest closed its mill in Youbou, near Dennis Cronin's hometown of Lake Cowichan, which had been in operation since 1913. The year before, the company announced it was increasing its raw log exports by 85 percent.

Raw logs—trees felled, limbed, and loaded onto a truck or ship for export without processing—are the most basic product that can be harvested from a forest. Such a base form of a resource holds the potential to have many more value-added layers. Processing the log into dimensional lumber is one; turning the waste into pulp products is another; and finally, the wood can be manufactured into high-value goods like furniture and guitars. Though some raw logs have been shipped abroad for as long as there has been commercial logging on Vancouver Island, throughout the twentieth century the majority of trees were processed at local mills into timber products that were then sold domestically and internationally. Some companies—such as Teal

Jones, which processes what it cuts on Vancouver Island at a mainland mill in Surrey, near Vancouver—have resisted the export of raw logs. Many other companies have not.

Any log removed from Crown land has to pass a surplus test: if the harvests exceed the needs of the province, then those surplus logs can be legally exported. The logs have to be put up for sale to provincial mills first, but if timber companies are no longer legally required to erect or maintain mills, there will be fewer places locally to buy and process logs. More and more wood, therefore, becomes surplus.

To Arnie Bercov, it's a "self-fulfilling prophecy." Bercov worked as a chokerman on a logging crew early in his career, before transitioning to work at a mill near Nanaimo and becoming president of the Public and Private Workers of Canada (PPWC), a union once known as the Pulp, Paper and Woodworkers of Canada. While some have blamed environmental movements for job losses and mill closures, Bercov has attributed the blame to government changes that have been undermining its most valuable industry.

Instead of employing thousands of mill workers and running dozens of production facilities, companies can simply export the wood and export the job. In 2016, the volume of raw logs exported from British Columbia had risen to 6.3 million cubic metres, which means that roughly one out of every three trees cut was shipped abroad—predominantly to China, Japan, and the United States—without any value added locally. Despite it being among the most renowned in the world, for every dollar of British Columbia timber, the province adds approximately thirty cents of value added, whereas Ontario and Quebec add $1.50. The province that once lured timber workers from across the country and turned remote communities into thriving towns has become one that places little value in the full potential of its resource.

But policies and practices of forestry companies themselves have also faced blame, above strictly environmental concerns. One Vancouver Island timber worker pointed to a flaw in the stumpage fee, the tax the provincial government levies based on volume of timber cut off Crown land. Some avaricious timber companies, when negotiating cutblocks with the provincial government, have been known to combine stands of valley-bottom old growth with those of a much lower value with no intention of cutting anything but the biggest and best. The government then calculates and charges a stumpage fee based on a considerably lower total average—and the company never cuts the less valuable stand, deceiving the government and maximizing profits.

AS TIMBER COMPANIES AND governments shifted the values they placed on British Columbia's forests, so too did the environmental movements. In the early 2000s, one environmental story dominated headlines: climate change. Activists were struggling to draw attention to massive global forces affecting the planet—the deterioration of the ozone layer, atmospheric carbon dioxide, rising ocean temperatures, acid rain—and local battles became dwarfed. On the coast, Western Canada Wilderness Committee activist Ken Wu watched as each environmental issue splintered and support began to be stretched thin. Wu felt that the ideological, social, or political needle towards ending old-growth forest logging wasn't moving.

Wu began his work as an activist canvassing in Vancouver for the WCWC during the Clayoquot Sound movement in the early 1990s. He was an ideological advocate for civil disobedience and blockades—a "serial protester," by his own definition. But a conversation during a car ride with WCWC co-founder Paul George lit a spark. George told him that while direct action—protesting, barricading logging roads, rallying—was an important component of environmental campaigns, the most crucial aspect was curating an educated and motivated public. Direct action can play a role, he told Wu, if it focuses the issue and drives people to action, but to change legislation requires considerable momentum and stamina in order to exert pressure on government. Their work wasn't just about bringing activists or even tourists into the forests, but to convince people—across the country and across the world—to care.

After two decades working as part of West Coast environmental movements, Wu found himself preaching to the converted and attracting few new acolytes. The organization's base was firmly established: a left-leaning, CBC-listening, Green Party–voting, environmentally conscious public. With the WCWC focused on shoring up its base and spreading its reach to cover new causes, including the expansion of oil pipelines to the coast and the proliferation of tankers, Wu saw an opportunity to expand into new demographics. He left the Western Canada Wilderness Committee to launch a new, forest-first organization.

On January 19, 2010, the Ancient Forest Alliance (AFA) was born. "The new organization will undertake expeditions to document the endangered ancient forests, heritage trees, and clear-cuts destroying the remaining old-growth forests on Vancouver Island and in southern B.C., and work to undertake public education and mobilization campaigns to ensure their protection," the organization's first statement read. The AFA was initially founded on four principal platforms: establish a provincial strategy to inventory the remaining old-growth forests; promote sustainable second-growth logging, including the retooling of mills to handle these logs; end the international export of raw logs to ensure local jobs are maintained; and support any Indigenous communities' land-use plans that focus on protecting old-growth forests.

The AFA was registered as a provincial non-profit society instead of a national charity, which allows it to openly support political parties and politicians who advocate old-growth protection—or condemn those who don't. The Western Canada Wilderness Committee, by contrast, holds charitable status, which allows them to speak in favour of or against policies but not vocally support parties or candidates. In effect, it means the Ancient Forest Alliance can be more overtly political. In its initial mandate, the organization stated it would "not be constrained by charitable status that forbids organizations from rejecting or endorsing politicians and parties due to their stances on important issues."

Wu's focus began to shift towards mobilizing a broader demographic. He started with an ambitious goal of expansion: to convince those British Columbians who typically put business or social interests above environmental ones to care about old-growth forest protection. He knew that he needed to break ground with three key groups: business owners, people of faith, and those of multicultural backgrounds. The rapidly growing Chinese and Indian communities in the Lower Mainland presented an opportunity for Wu to captivate a new generation of Canadians, many of whom became enamoured of British Columbia's big nature. Wu, who is of Taiwanese descent, began offering big-tree tours in Mandarin. Likewise, he figured people of faith who were part of the growing trend away from structured religion to a more broad spirituality might find resonance within the forests. Activities including "nature therapy" and "forest bathing"—immersing oneself in a forest as a tool for healing, stress relief, and mindfulness—were on the rise. Taking a walk in the woods became a spiritual act, a way to connect with forces greater than the individual.

But it was the business groups that proposed the greatest challenge and the greatest reward. Wu saw that if a movement is purely based on ideals that are divorced from the economy, it will never be seen as anything other than an echo chamber. But if he could connect the two, if people's livelihoods were at stake, they would fight as hard and as passionately as the ideologues and idealists. The obstacle was changing the minds of people who have for generations relied, culturally and financially, on timber rather than trees.

For many British Columbians, the battles for Carmanah and Clayoquot felt like a lifetime ago and an issue more or less settled—the wars were won and the old growth was saved. The cause was fading from media and public attention. Being in emergency mode all the time is not only exhausting—for activists as well as supporters—but unsustainable. This palpable sense of fatigue brought rise to one of the more fundamental shifts, both organizationally and personally, for Wu. The Ancient Forest Alliance needed to focus not just on the negatives—clear-cutting, job losses, ecological impacts—but on the positives. Wu realized he needed to focus on what he and the AFA were in favour of, rather than hammering on about what they stood against. There had to be green among the grey. His fledgling organization needed to find and document the remaining exceptionally large trees and intact stands, and bring evidence of what was at stake into people's homes. These remaining trees and groves, rather than stumps and clear-cuts, would be the spark that would reignite the movement.

His first hire was twenty-five-year-old photographer TJ Watt, who Wu had previously contracted to take pictures of protests and forests for WCWC campaigns. Watt was born in Metchosin, a leafy coastal community just outside Victoria, close to the location of some of the island's first logging mills. When he was a kid, he would climb a large cedar in the backyard of his house until he could see over the rooftops. Watt's father told him that the forest behind the house, which looked so wild, had once been logged. It took a moment, but then Watt saw it: springboard notches and an old logging road. It was the first time he saw historical layers in a forest.

In high school, Watt grew interested in photography, buying disposable cameras at the gas station with Petro-Points. After earning a diploma in professional photography at the Western Academy of Photography in Victoria, he joined the AFA as a campaigner and photographer with the principal job of seeking out old-growth forests, big trees, and recent clear-cuts. Photography was a tried-and-tested method of raising awareness for an environmental cause, but there were new tools that had appeared on the scene since Ken Wu had campaigned in Carmanah and Clayoquot, including social media.

"You can find the trees," Wu said, "but you have to know how to market them."

Half of Ken Wu's job at the AFA is spent trying to draw attention, trying to sell the forests and sell the trees. He hired Watt to find them.

IN DECEMBER 2009, a month before the Ancient Forest Alliance was established, TJ Watt grabbed his camera and headed into the forests of southern Vancouver Island. He went to photograph the Walbran Valley, a region that had been a focal point of environmental activism since the early 1990s. As a self-proclaimed "big-tree hunter," even while not on assignment for the AFA he would still spend free weekends hiking and exploring. Watt had been to the Walbran before, but this excursion was his first of many into the bush with the express purpose of locating old-growth forests that stood awaiting the saw. After a night sleeping in his Subaru with a friend, with temperatures dropping to where his socks froze to the windows, he decided to take the backroads south in the direction of Port Renfrew. Hillsides were patched with clear-cuts, some containing enormous cedar stumps, and most of the forests he passed—even stands that towered above his vehicle—were second growth.

He checked his map, noticing that he was in the Gordon River Valley just outside of town. As the winter sun was beginning to set, something caught Watt's eye: grey spikes sticking out above the canopy of the forest along the logging road. While many forests in central and eastern Canada undergo a radical and all-consuming colour shift, turning a riotous spectrum of reds, oranges, and yellows in the fall, the forests of Vancouver Island remain predominantly green year round. But within this unwavering colour, hills of old-growth Pacific temperate rainforest appear variegated and motley. The canopy is dappled: dark green for the conifers (the firs and hemlocks and cedars), and lighter for the deciduous (the maples and alders). From a distance, it is often hard to tell a five-hundred-year-old forest from one that is seventy-five years old. But there is one clear marker of Pacific temperate old-growth forest: the spiky, dead tops of ancient cedars. These multi-tipped crowns—known as candelabra tops—are a characteristic of age. When a cedar is several hundred years old, its fragile tip often breaks off in fierce wind or from a lightning strike. From the fractured top sprout new branches that turn skywards, and after decades these often dry out and die themselves. The spiky crowns become bleached grey in the sun, and stand out from the dark green conifer forest like splintered popsicle sticks.

Watt knew what to look for, and here, along the side of the road, multiple candelabra tops emerged from the dark green foliage. He parked his car and scrambled down a slope into the forest. Almost instantly, he came across an enormous, burly cedar and a towering Douglas fir, both with tops protruding through the well-established canopy. For a region that had seen extensive logging for the better part of a century, it shocked Watt that a stand of old growth containing valuable timber not only still stood so close to Port Renfrew, but also alongside a well-used logging road. Within an hour, he had located more than a dozen trees three to four metres wide—some with great twisted forms and burls erupting from their bases.

Knowing Ken Wu would be interested, Watt returned to Victoria and went straight to the seasoned activist to tell him of his find. Wu initially didn't believe that a grove of old-growth forest stood fifteen minutes from Port Renfrew. He had to see it for himself. Around a month later, when the pair found time to drive up the coast from Victoria to Port Renfrew, Wu was dumbfounded at the size of some of the trees and the density of the grove. But while they were walking through the forest, something jumped out at Watt. Scattered throughout the grove hung the familiar orange "FALLING BOUNDARY" and pink "ROAD LOCATION" ribbons placed by Teal Jones's forest engineers. Large cedars were marked with spray paint, identifying the largest trees in the cutblock or other markings for the fallers. Within the short period between his visits, timber engineers had been sent to flag the forest and lay out a cutblock map. To Watt and Wu, it was a clear sign that the company intended to return with fallers and trucks and turn this patch of old growth into a familiar grey sight.

The Ancient Forest Alliance had found its inaugural ancient forest.

Weeks after the organization's founding, the AFA issued a press release that announced a new battleground for the fight to protect old-growth forests on Vancouver Island. They called it Avatar Grove, after the James Cameron sci-fi epic that had been released just months prior and was already starting to break box-office records. Beneath the flare of 3-D filmmaking was a not so thinly veiled message: it is possible to fight back against a company that is exploiting land and extracting resources without regard for Indigenous peoples or the environment.

Twentieth Century Fox had been taken aback by the strong ecological message in the draft script of *Avatar.* "When they read it, they sort of said, 'Can we take some of this tree-hugging, *FernGully* crap out of this movie?'" director James Cameron said in an interview. "And I said, 'No, because that's why I'm making the film.'"

In addition to identifying with the film's environmental message, the AFA likened the unusually shaped cedars found in Avatar Grove to some of the alien trees growing on Cameron's fictional moon Pandora. It was also a catchy name—one that would resonate with the public and attract the attention of the media. To further link *Avatar*'s environmental message to their cause, the AFA held a rally in Vancouver where dozens of participants painted their bodies blue in emulation of the Na'vi, Cameron's forest-dwelling aliens. The organization even invited the famous director to attend, but he didn't show up.

It was the second time Ken Wu had used pop culture as a conduit for a pro-environment protest. In 2004, while working for the Western Canada Wilderness

Committee, he organized a rally at the B.C. legislature in Victoria—the largest at that location since the Clayoquot Sound protest in 1993—where participants dressed in papier-mâché costumes of Ents, the giant tree creatures from J. R. R. Tolkien's *Lord of the Rings* trilogy. The protestors acted out a battle against dark forces that were destroying the forests.

During the wave of West Coast forest activism that began in the 1980s, names for big trees and groves were bestowed principally based on location. In Randy Stoltmann's pioneering book, *Hiking Guide to the Big Trees of Southwestern British Columbia*, his descriptions of some of the province's grandest groves shy away from flash or glamorous identification. Trees held names such as the San Juan Spruce, Red Creek Fir, or Lynn Creek Cedar, as well as many with Indigenous roots such as Carmanah, Koksilah, and Cheewhat.

More recent activist organizations have felt that aggressive marketing is needed in order to turn these trees into symbols. Organizations such as the Ancient Forest Alliance don't have the luxury of being timid. They must create a splash.

"Avatar Grove would probably be a sea of stumps right now had we called it Gordon River Valley Grove," said Ken Wu. "If you don't know how to build a communications campaign around them, then they're just another big tree, ultimately."

But not everyone views the marketing of these big trees and old-growth groves as positive. One central point of tension is the language used in some environmental activist campaigns, primarily around the word "discovery." Indigenous people point to their history on the land—long before any timber worker or activist—and the evidence that can be found in the markings and remnants of culturally modified trees. Activist organizations often defend the language by saying that their "discovery" is not to say they were the first to ever see the tree or walk the grove, but that they are the first to recognize the tourism or recreation potential and significance of the trees.

The naming of places has always been a fraught process in Canada, where thousands of years of Indigenous history and presence have been erased by placing a single word on a map. It is a subject that splits Vancouver Island's environmental activist community, with each organization trying to push forcibly for results while being cautious not to step on cultural toes. For some, naming groves or trees after Western movies or literature applies yet another layer of Western presence on Indigenous land. The text on the wooden sign at the trailhead to Avatar Grove includes "T'l'oqwxwat"—the Pacheedaht name for the site of a long-time summer fishing camp along the Gordon River. But the Indigenous word has never found its way into colloquial usage.

"They were 'finding' something that's well documented within Pacheedaht history and likely has a name and likely has uses," said Kristine Pearson, a representative for the First Nation. And the propensity to label the forests with a Western name has never sat well either. "It would be one thing if you came to the nation first and asked about the history," she said. "It's a very colonial attitude to come in and rename an area."

Avatar Grove was more than just marketing: the forest contained some three- and four-metre-wide cedars that were easily several hundred years old. The AFA declared it "the most accessible and finest stand of ancient trees left in a wilderness setting on the South Island." To Ken Wu and TJ Watt, the forest held everything they needed to create a tourist destination. Places like Carmanah or Walbran or the islands of Clayoquot Sound are the cream of Vancouver Island's old-growth forests, but their remote locations, down dozens of kilometres of logging roads, act as a deterrent to most. People are less inclined to visit one—even to view the largest tree in the country—if it's a three-hour drive down bumpy, tire-flattening roads, or if it requires bushwhacking on foot or taking a boat across a choppy channel. Avatar Grove lay just beyond where the pavement ends, an easy drive outside Port Renfrew. With minimal effort, visitors could explore a prime example of untouched Pacific temperate rainforest. They could also see first-hand what is in danger of being lost, without having to delve deep into Vancouver Island's interior. The value in Avatar Grove—not only from an ecological or tourism perspective, but for the AFA's cause—was as staggeringly obvious as the towering trees.

The subsequent press releases caught the attention of the media, who were eager for stories about a new war in the woods, or at least a fresh skirmish. With British Columbia's history of timber and forest activism, a rapt audience was guaranteed. "I know that we would've succeeded in building a powerful movement anyways, but Avatar Grove was rocket fuel," Wu said.

On a spring day, after showing reporters the forest, Watt and Wu decided to check out the north side of the road, where another patch of old growth extended up a hill. As they hiked through the salal undergrowth, they passed even more giant cedars, one after another. Then, as they crossed Baird Creek, a seasonal trickle of water that flows into the Gordon River, Watt spotted something up a hill: an enormous, stout, burly cedar. While western red cedars can grow straight and branchless, with a grain eloquent enough for guitar making or true enough for canoe building, the aged examples of the species are known for more erratic and misshapen growth. After hundreds of years, the centres of cedar trunks often rot away, leaving hollow cavities that offer ideal dens for a family of black bears. On some cedars, the grain twists and turns, creating folds and mounds in the bark that from some angles make the trees look like sitting Buddhas meditating in a forest.

Most of the ancient cedars in Avatar Grove were impressive in their girth and stature, but this one tree was so unusual in its shape that the activists knew they had found this forest's protagonist. The cedar appeared squashed by some unseen force from above that was pushing bulbous lumps out from its base. A few metres off the ground, a burl the size of a small car protruded from the trunk like a giant's goiter. Cedar burls were once thought to be an infection in the bark or some kind of arboreal tumour, but recently the protruding lumps have been thought to be stores of regenerative cells that a tree can access when it is damaged in the wind—when its top is broken or its trunk split. Some burls swell and shrink over time.

The cedar growing on the slope in Avatar Grove wasn't the largest or tallest, but it broke the mould for how a tree should look. So the AFA presented the specimen to the world as "the gnarliest tree in Canada." The organization suggested having an online vote or competition to name the unusual tree, but "Canada's Gnarliest Tree"—or more colloquially, "the Gnarly Tree"—stuck. The campaign to save Avatar Grove exploded like wildfire. To TJ Watt, the movement was beginning to feel like a "mini Carmanah." Everything was coming together: the exceptionality of the stand of giant trees, the accessibility of the short drive from Port Renfrew, and the fact that an environmentally minded blockbuster movie was breaking box-office records in theatres. It was the perfect moment to launch a powerful pro–old-growth forest campaign.

THE ANCIENT FOREST ALLIANCE led its first hike through Avatar Grove that same spring, guiding nearly a hundred people through the rain and bush. The organization set a goal of leading at least one hike every month for a year. People who could see first-hand the size and rarity of these trees were key to spreading the word and furthering the cause. Still, every time TJ Watt drove over the bump separating pavement and dirt logging road on a visit to Avatar Grove, he felt anxiety build in him. He didn't know if one day he would turn his van around the final corner and find the trees he was working to protect had been cut and hauled away. They needed to find a way to ensure this patch of forest was officially off limits to logging.

At first, the move to protect a small patch of old-growth forest was met with a familiar tepid response from the provincial government. "I think it is important to mention that not all old-growth forests can be protected," wrote Pat Bell, the British Columbia minister of forests and range, in response to a letter from the Sooke Region Tourism Association and Port Renfrew Chamber of Commerce, which extolled the broader economic benefits of leaving old-growth forests that held recreation values. "A certain amount must be harvested to provide a viable and sustainable wood supply to the forest industry, which is an important component of the provincial economy."

As news began to circulate more widely about Avatar Grove, writer and former environmental auditor Hans Tammemagi drove out to see the forest in the summer of 2010. He was shocked that an old-growth forest or a five-hundred-year-old tree held no formal protection. Those within parks or protected areas did, but the trees carried no weight in and of themselves. Tammemagi continued farther up the Gordon River Valley to a recent clear-cut that contained several cedar stumps approximately three metres wide. One stump was nearly five metres in diameter—nearly wide enough for three people of average height to lie head to toe across its cut. Harvested that spring, cutblock 7184 lay just down the road from 7190, which was awaiting a pair of forest engineers to lay out its cutting map.

For Tammemagi, who had worked in and around forestry issues in Canada for decades, the contrast between the intact forest and recent clear-cuts was staggering.

When he called the office of the logging company that held the tree farm license, Teal Jones, they were adamant that what they had done was entirely legal. They had submitted a cutting application to the ministry, received approval, and set to work. There existed no legal mechanism or requirement for timber companies to save or exclude big trees. They may set aside a bear den here or there, or extend a riparian zone, but it is done at the discretion of the forest engineers.

In June 2010, Tammemagi filed a complaint to the Forest Practices Board (FPB), the province's independent watchdog for forest and forestry issues. Formed in the wake of the Forest Practices Code of British Columbia Act, which came into effect in 1995, the board's responsibilities included ensuring the act was being followed; reviewing complaints and conducting audits into forest and range practices; and issuing reports and recommendations to the provincial government. The FPB received nineteen complaints within the first year of its establishment. Tammemagi's demands were threefold: a full stop on cutting the most "ancient" trees, a long-term strategy to protect old growth, and the immediate safeguarding of Avatar Grove from logging.

In their report, released in February 2011, the Forest Practices Board highlighted a number of problematic issues, including the fact that forest policy "does not classify old growth in a sufficiently refined way to capture the full range of old forest values." A forest that is 250 years old is treated the same way as one that is more than 500 years old. Similarly, a tree that is 250 years old is treated the same way as one that is a thousand years old. If they're not protected in a provincial park, wildlife habitat zone, or old-growth management area, the most ancient and rare of Vancouver Island's trees can simply be cut.

The FPB recognized that "certain individual, or small groups of, exceptional trees on the timber harvesting land base may provide a higher social and economic value if they are treated as a special resource feature and excluded from timber harvesting." Teal Jones responded to the board that these larger trees are often dying or rotten and are consequently felled not for timber value but as a safety measure for its employees working in the field. In its recommendations, the FPB encouraged "government, forest professionals, and forest licensees to seek creative means to conserve trees of exceptional size or form, age or historical significance and, where appropriate, the forest stands that contain them." It was a move that excited pro–old-growth environmentalists.

The Forest Practices Board submitted their report to minister of forests and range Pat Bell, who requested a review of the government's existing legal mechanisms to protect big trees. The review determined that the tools and processes—the formation of old-growth management areas or recreation sites, for example—were only sufficient when the big trees were identified prior to the onset of logging operations in the area. No legal process required timber companies to set aside a thousand-year-old tree, for example, once harvesting had begun. Nor was there a mechanism for the provincial government to intervene once operations were underway. The pressure was placed on the public—activists, environmentalists, hikers, and the like—to find and identify these monumental trees before the process was initiated.

When the province opened up a public review process, 232 out of 236 comments submitted were in favour of protecting Avatar Grove. Under public pressure, Minister Pat Bell called Ken Wu and set up a meeting. Bell made it clear to the activists that broad legislation to halt old-growth logging was not on the table. But setting aside Avatar Grove—the small patch just outside Port Renfrew—was.

The AFA's request was straightforward: a small protected area along Baird Creek could be extended to encompass the entire grove. The thin band had been designated an old-growth management area (OGMA), a patch of forest recognized by the provincial government to contain old-growth attributes. Some OGMAS are intact groves untouched by commercial logging, while others are younger second-growth stands that are off limits to logging and maintained to achieve old-growth characteristics. There are more than fifty thousand OGMAS around the province, representing nearly four million hectares of forested land, but an investigation in 2010 by the Forest Practices Board found that approximately 30 percent of these OGMAS had protection by a government order, while 70 percent held no legal status—likely a result of government land-use plans acting not as legal requirements but as guidelines. Timber companies could build roads through or even harvest two-thirds of OGMAS. However, in their investigation, the board found that most licensees tended to avoid all OGMAS, even though they were not legally required to. Still, that the responsibility to protect forests is largely to the discretion of the logging industry left activists uneasy.

Following negotiations, the minister agreed to extend the protected area to cover the entirety of what the activists were asking for, creating a fifty-nine-hectare old-growth management area. In February 2012, two years to the month after the AFA announced its identification of the old-growth stand, Avatar Grove was officially given protected status.

The gnarly cedars within this patch of forest had found their shield—but safety came at a cost. To appease Teal Jones, which was now out of a lease to cut approximately sixty hectares of forest, Pat Bell offered compensation in exchange, by adjusting the borders of existing OGMAS to open them up for logging. Half of this compensation consisted of forest more than 250 years old, and half of older second growth, including one area of approximately one-hundred-year-old Douglas firs—a rarity on Vancouver Island.

Just outside Lake Cowichan, a three-thousand-person town northeast of Port Renfrew in the middle of Vancouver Island, Mark Carter was running Teal Jones's operations for tree farm licence 46 out of a small trailer office, managing the company's forest engineers, including Dennis Cronin. Carter described the deal with Avatar Grove as an "easy call." Even though the Ancient Forest Alliance said in early 2010 that "the Grove is slated for logging any day now," representatives for Teal Jones have tempered this claim. When the company sent in their timber cruisers to do a value assessment, the cutblock didn't register as anything exceptionally significant—particularly in a region that contained sections of forests of much higher value. There were large cedars, but they were old, misshapen, or broken. The land was uneven, too, sloping down a mountainside with many gullies and depressions, which would make it more difficult to fell and extract than other patches in the valley. Carter called the deal a "win-win," where the AFA received a grove of old growth within a short drive from Port Renfrew that they could market and publicize to tourists, and the logging company received stands of higher-commercial-value timber farther from town. Still, the deal was a tough pill to swallow for the activists, and a precedent Ken Wu felt uncomfortable setting. With so little of Vancouver Island protected in parks or old-growth management areas, and so much of it fragmented and disconnected, every stand of old growth or older second growth counts.

IN THE TWO YEARS after Avatar Grove was first announced, thousands of people hiked the forest, creating two paths: one leading to TJ Watt's Gnarly Tree in the upper half of the grove, and another in a loop around the largest trees of the lower half. But the only way into the grove was for visitors to haul themselves up a slippery, often muddy slope, using a rope. It was a less than an ideal—or safe—entry point to what was becoming the West Coast's new *it*-forest. The need to establish a more official trail system grew.

In the summer of 2013, the Ancient Forest Alliance received confirmation from the B.C. Ministry of Forests, Lands and Natural Resource Operations that Avatar Grove would be an official recreation site, and permission was given to begin constructing a formal trail. The Pacheedaht First Nation donated cedar planks for the first phase of a boardwalk, which was expanded to include a number of viewing platforms and benches.

But the First Nation was also not without concerns, pointing to the lack of toilet and refuse facilities, which are often found in provincial parks and managed by parks services. More importantly, Jeff Jones, chief of the Pacheedaht, pointed to a missed or yet-to-be-developed opportunity: there is nobody more experienced and knowledgeable about these forests than the Indigenous people who have lived, used, and worked within them for millennia. He said the Ancient Forest Alliance initially suggested that during the summer high season, a permanent representative of the First Nation would offer guided walks through Avatar Grove, providing information both historical and ecological, and diminishing the impact of tourists who might otherwise wander off trail. With limited funding, guides have yet to be hired.

The AFA has also received criticism from some who point to the thousands of tourists traipsing through a once-pristine old-growth forest as a mark of hypocrisy. If these organizations are truly for the protection of sensitive and dwindling forests, then why allow hordes of tourists to trample the undergrowth and clamber up the burls of trees to take photographs? It is an argument that Ken Wu easily dismisses: a thin trail through the forest is a small measure of impact compared to what might have befallen the grove. And with time, the impact of the initial hikers and the construction workers will fade. Some of the first boardwalks built in Carmanah Walbran Provincial Park in the mid-1990s have slowly been enveloped by the forest green, to the point where traversing the walkways in Carmanah feels like strolling on top of a cloud of undergrowth without disturbing anything living. Given time to heal, nature will reassert its dominance.

Following Avatar Grove, the AFA announced the identification of two other groves in the region that also held potential as tourist destinations. The first was a section of old-growth forest, seventy hectares of which was a protected wildlife habitat, while another sixty hectares lay within a tree farm licence with no protection. Off Highway 14, just south of Port Renfrew on the road to Victoria, down a path frequented by in-the-know surfers heading to a secluded beach, was a grove of ancient cedars, firs, and spruces tightly clustered like the monoliths of Stonehenge. When it came to adding a name, Ken Wu knew exactly what to call it—a name that he had been looking to attach to a stand of old growth for years: Jurassic Grove. Plus, as the organization stated, if the British Columbia government decided to expand nearby Juan de Fuca Provincial Park to include the grove, the area could be renamed Jurassic Park.

The second location featured centuries-old Sitka spruces rather than the bulbous western red cedars of Avatar Grove. One spruce was nearly four metres in diameter, almost big enough to break into the top-ten widest known Sitka spruces in the province. TJ Watt called the grove the "Serengeti of Vancouver Island" because of its biodiversity of fauna—elk, black bears, and wolves. The AFA named it FernGully Grove, after *FernGully: The Last Rainforest*—the 1992 animated film that centres around an alliance between fairies and animals as they fight to protect the destruction of their forest from loggers and an evil entity bent on its eradication.

Still, not every campaign took off like Avatar Grove. A few kilometres farther into the Gordon River Valley lay a section of old-growth forest that rivalled any in the region. It held big trees and bear dens, bubbling streams and waterfalls. The AFA nicknamed it the Christy Clark Grove, after the then premier of British Columbia who, after being elected in 2011, had shown little interest in shifting policy away from old-growth logging. The organization even named one of the grove's largest Douglas firs the Clark Giant, and a burly western red cedar the Gnarly Clark, thinking that the premier couldn't let trees named after her be cut down. It was a bid to draw the attention of the province's highest politician to these vanishing forests, but the campaign never got off the ground. The name confused some left-leaning supporters, who accused Ken Wu of honouring the British Columbia Liberal premier instead of singling the politician out. The AFA eventually renamed the premier's unwanted eponymous forest the more tame and apolitical Eden Grove.

It wasn't the first time an environmental activist had tried this tactic with little success. In the summer of 1988, Randy Stoltmann found a Sitka spruce in the Carmanah Valley that had one of the largest circumferences he had ever come across. The tree was dead, a standing snag, so he named it the Dave Parker Tree after the minister of forests who had called the forests of Carmanah "over-mature" and therefore of little value and in need of immediate harvesting. The name never stuck.

Public attention on its own can rarely lead to formal protection for these forests. For each of the AFA's identified ancient groves near Port Renfrew, Ken Wu tried to court the Pacheedaht First Nation, who he said has held the "trump card on the issue" of pushing for protection. In some instances, support was forthcoming—from supplying wood for boardwalks to lobbying the government—while in others the Pacheedaht have been cautious about wholly taking the activists' side. Support from the nation meant that the activists wouldn't have to engage in any direct-action forms of protest or hold rallies. Instead, the Pacheedaht could push for the groves to be turned into old-growth management areas in their negotiations with timber companies. That way, the AFA wouldn't have to make concessions to the

British Columbia government as they did with Avatar Grove, trading nine cutblocks to save one.

AVATAR GROVE ARRIVED AT a time of widespread skepticism and doubt within the environmental community in Canada. Three months after the AFA's flagship forest was formally protected, the country's elder of environmentalism, David Suzuki, was struck with defeatism. "Environmentalism has failed," he boldly declared in May 2012. He cited many successes, but noted that "we were so focused on battling opponents and seeking public support that we failed to realize these battles reflect fundamentally different ways of seeing our place in the world." But within this handful of hectares of old-growth forest near Port Renfrew was an optimistic model of collaboration among activists and timber workers, Indigenous groups and businesses.

Still, not everyone immediately swooned at the tourism potential of marketing Vancouver Island's big trees. Greg Klem, who moved to Port Renfrew from Kitchener, Ontario, in the mid-1990s, had driven by what became Avatar Grove many times while working in tree planting, up and down Vancouver Island—part of the hordes of seasonal workers contributing to the 200 million seedlings that are planted every year across the province.

Klem was surprised by the attention Avatar Grove was receiving. In his estimation, the stand wasn't even that special. He had walked through dozens of old-growth groves that were grander and more varied than the one attracting the media and the public. The forest, according to him, is based on a lie—he claims it is not entirely old growth but a handful of ancient cedars interspersed with much younger hemlocks, which led him to dub it "Avafraud Grove."

In an opinion article for the *Sooke News Mirror,* a local paper, in the spring of 2011, Klem wrote, "Unfortunately, much of the campaign has been based on misinformation, falsehoods and 'spin.' The 'Avatar Grove' is neither ancient nor endangered. The handful of damaged, old survivors are surrounded by 100-year-old diseased hemlock that grew after a major windstorm." He wrote that there were other forests in the area that were more spectacular than Avatar but were logged without fanfare or opposition, noting that "some trees must be more equal" than others, in a reference to George Orwell's *Animal Farm*.

The Ancient Forest Alliance defended their campaign by focusing on Avatar Grove's location, saying it is "particularly valuable because it is the easiest to access monumental stand of ancient trees near Port Renfrew. Other old-growth stands are farther away along rough logging roads, on steep slopes."

While forests untouched by commercial logging may not bear the scars of chainsaws or heavy machinery, they still demonstrate natural wounds. No old-growth forest on Vancouver Island stands utterly unblemished, with every tree being allowed to grow unmolested. There are always young trees alongside the ancients.

But Klem's frustration had a deeper cause. These forests had formed the foundation of an eco-tour company that he had casually established a decade before Avatar Grove was brought into the limelight. He would explain logging practices and history to visitors, all the while driving the bumpy backroads more often frequented by hulking trucks laden with logs than tourists. He would point out big trees, but also big clear-cuts. He would guide groups through old growth while explaining the problems with today's timber harvesting. He would show the grey as well as the green.

The centre point of his tour was a massive, twisted cedar that he nicknamed "Lumpy," a tree whose location he has kept a relative secret—rather than publicizing the tree for anyone else or any organization to use for their benefit. On the side of his white pickup truck he scrawled in green paint his email address, in case a passerby might be interested in a Lumpy Tour. But Klem's exasperation boiled as he saw the attention on TJ Watt's "Gnarliest Tree in Canada" grow from local to national—with hundreds of visitors on busy summer weekends clambering into the forest to see the unusual tree. "It's not even the twelfth-gnarliest in the district," Klem said, without offering examples or recognizing the complete subjectivity of the designation. To make a point, Klem retrieved his can of green paint, and along the tailgate of his truck wrote a new slogan for his Lumpy Tours: "Bigger. Better. Knarlier [*sic*]."

Once Avatar Grove started to pick up momentum as a focus for tourists—and the AFA began giving free hiking tours—Klem found it harder to compete to the point where his business dried up. He has no Instagram page or fancy website; his only advertising is a small listing in the business directory in the Port Renfrew Chamber of Commerce's brochure. Rather than polished activist-speak, he'll give you a reality check from someone not shy with the contradictions: that some of the highest-productivity forest regions are also where we have built our communities; that a gradual weaning away from old-growth logging is more likely than a cold-turkey full stop; and that environmentalists will always look to polish a feature in order to market their cause.

Klem has been imagining a reality show based on the premise of hunting Canada's next biggest trees. "More than likely you'll find it right on Mount Edinburgh, in that goshawk preserve," he said, speaking about the mountain that rises above the Gordon River Valley. "There's giants in there."

The elusive big trees that may stand somewhere within a remote valley on Vancouver Island have always inspired Klem to seek them out. There is power in stumbling upon a natural skyscraper in a dark forest—maybe not power to push change, but at the very least power to inspire. "Fewer people are going to church anymore, so they're looking for something to grasp on to. Forests is the new cause for them."

For the Ancient Forest Alliance, encouraging tourists to visit Avatar Grove was out of hope that each person would come away with an impression—awe at the very least, vexation that these forests are still being cut at best, and ideally something approaching anger that could be harnessed into action. But mostly, people come to see the trees. They come to wander in the woods and look up at the towering Douglas firs and take photographs beside the plump western red cedars, their tiny frames juxtaposed with some of the largest examples of these species on the planet. It is the story of the trees that people are drawn to.

While the organization was writing press release after press release and feverishly petitioning the provincial government to protect Avatar Grove, timber workers continued to delve deeper into the valleys of Vancouver Island, flagging and cutting hundreds of other patches of old-growth forest. In late January 2011, a few kilometres down the dirt road from Avatar Grove and across a bridge high over the Gordon River, Dennis Cronin stepped out of his truck, quietly put on his caulk boots and hard hat, and began preparations to bring down cutblock 7190.

CHAPTER 7

The Logger

DENNIS CRONIN STEPPED BACK from the giant Douglas fir he had just flagged with green ribbon, and continued on through the forest. As he was marking the cutblock with orange and pink and red ribbons, he noticed he was being followed. It was common to encounter a bear in these remote valleys; cougars and wolves were more rare. But this time it was a bird. Wherever he went in the cutblock, a blue and black Steller's jay—the official bird of British Columbia—took particular interest in his work.

"He would follow me around like a dog," Cronin later said. "I would be traversing creeks, taking my measurements and bearings, and he's hopping behind me, picking up the bugs as I stirred them up."

The bird would stop when he stopped, cock its crested head to the side, and follow along. Even when he returned the following day to finish the site plan, at some point the jay would appear and Cronin would toss a piece of his peanut butter sandwich to the bird. But when Cronin and his partner, Walter Van Hell, found a way over the creek that acted as the boundary of 7190 to flag a neighbouring section of old growth, the jay stopped. As the pair completed their work in the two cutblocks near the base of Edinburgh Mountain in the Gordon River Valley, traversing back and forth across the creek boundary, the bird always remained in 7190.

"He would never cross that creek. We would pick him up again when we crossed back," Cronin said.

At the Teal Jones office, a teal-coloured office located fifty kilometres away from cutblock 7190, near Lake Cowichan, Cronin and Van Hell transcribed their field notes of the forest's features and contours on a computer map of the cutblock. They added thin red lines for the creeks and rivers, to mirror the red flagging they had placed in the forest. They marked where an access point should be built, where a cable yarder could be positioned to haul the logs to the road. And they calculated the merchantable cubic metres of wood within the cutblock. At roughly the size of twelve football fields, cutblock 7190 was a tiny sliver of the great forests that had once covered the island. But it held some towering and valuable trees. The price of timber fluctuates every year, depending on species and market, but that year, old growth was fetching between $80 and $100 per cubic metre of wood. (One cubic metre is roughly the size of a telephone pole.) West Coast old-growth forests produce between 800 and 1,200 cubic metres of wood per hectare, roughly twice as much timber as second growth.

The gross value of the wood in this one cutblock could yield approximately one million dollars.

DENNIS CRONIN SPENT THE majority of his life walking through old-growth forests, under the canopies of some of the largest trees in the country. He was born in the spring of 1954 in Toronto, and his family moved out of the city when he was five. In 1972, when he was eighteen years old and living in the small farming town of Whitby, Ontario, he headed west, where he had a choice of towns on Vancouver Island which were booming under the banner of falling trees. At the time, the West Coast timber industry was raging, with big money to be made. Unlike other resource surges across the country—in oil production, mining, or seasonal fishing—the move to work in the forests was more often than not a permanent one. Towns across the island had sprouted out of the sawdust of timber mills. Work camps situated in remote locations in the bush had evolved into communities with schools, shops, post offices, and hospitals. Holding everything together was the local timber company, which provided jobs and incomes to keep families not only afloat but flourishing. Some towns, such as Mill Bay on the east coast of the island, bear names that reflect their timber history.

For Cronin, a secure job was only half the draw. He wanted to work in the great outdoors of British Columbia, with pitch on his hands and mud on his jeans. He settled in the tranquil community of Lake Cowichan. The town was not only located in the heart of southern Vancouver Island's forested hills but for decades had been one of the region's most important timber hubs. For a decade and a half, through the heyday of West Coast logging, Cronin walked the forests as a hooktender, leading a crew that hauled logs out of cutblocks. "It was continuous clear-cut back then," Cronin said. "You just cut everything down. If it was there, you mowed 'er all down."

As the eastern half of Vancouver Island began to run out of the high-value, old-growth forests so coveted by timber companies, operations started delving into the plunging and wet valleys of the island's west coast. "I logged some big dough in the valleys," said Cronin, with both a touch of pride and a touch of regret. "You'd only be six hundred feet from the landing and there'd be just monsters." In the sluice flats of the Nitinat Valley, west of Cowichan Lake and up the coast from Port Renfrew, he remembered Sitka spruces so big they defied standard operation. "You'd have to get low beds to come in," he said. "You couldn't get the logs high enough to get them onto a logging truck. You'd need two machines picking it up at the same time."

In the late 1980s, after years of back-breaking work hauling logs, Cronin wanted a change. The B.C. government was formalizing the role of forest engineers and they recognized his experience, like that of many others, and counted it as training. It was a calmer job, and one less taxing on the body.

Forest engineers are often the first wave of loggers to enter a cutblock. Their job is to survey the land, design where roads should go, mark any unusual features, and build a layout map for the fallers. "We might walk around for three days scratching our heads, looking at the ground, looking at the trees," Cronin said. In this role, he began seeing trees differently. "Fallers see them lying on the ground, not standing up," he said. "So it's quite a difference being the first ones in." In his previous role, he worked in cutblocks that had been clear-cut, but as an engineer he worked in intact forests untouched by commercial logging.

In the bush, Cronin looked every bit of a West Coast logger. When he went to work, he wore jeans and a plaid or work shirt, with the sleeves rolled up when the weather was warm. He wore a hard hat and a timberman's spike-soled caulk boots so he could traverse the forest with ease. He shaved clean, except for a bushy moustache. He never left for work without a loaf of bread and a jar of peanut butter for his lunch.

For fifteen years, he had one main partner while working in the woods of Vancouver Island, forest engineer Walter Van Hell. The pair became so comfortable in the bush that when they came across a bear den in a hollow cavity of a large cedar tree, they would reach inside and feel around, or even poke their heads in, without any fear that a bear would come tearing out or tear something off.

Cronin didn't just work the forest; he lived and breathed the bush. Few weekends passed without at least one excursion into the vast network of unpaved logging roads around Lake Cowichan or Port Renfrew. He would go hunting up the mountains with friends, or fishing with his two sons along the hundreds of creeks and rivers that drain into the Pacific. One of his favourite activities was shed-antler hunting, where he would hike around looking for deer or elk racks that the animals would naturally drop in early spring. Or he would simply wake up on a Saturday morning and say to his wife, Lorraine, "Come and see my new patch," which referred to either a grove of old growth he had recently flagged or a forest that had recently been cut.

They would often hop in their truck and head out for the day, to hike through a grove Cronin had been working or to a point of interest—maybe it was a sliver of Pacific Ocean that had recently been exposed after loggers had done work to a cutblock. Maybe it was a bear den. Or maybe it was a tree he deemed unusual.

Over decades, Cronin developed a deep understanding of these forests. There were some who just went to work and got the job done, but Cronin wanted to know the details. He could recite the names of every species in the rainforest and the regulations within the governing codes. When his co-workers had a question, they would seek out Dennis.

Cronin had seen hundreds of giants, but this one Douglas fir in cutblock 7190 stood above the rest. "When I walked up to it, I passed some big firs and some really big cedars—twelve-footers, maybe," Cronin said, referring to the diameter of neighbouring trees. But this one fir dominated the rest. "He towered above the forest. He stuck out like a sore thumb."

Douglas firs and western red cedar are the two species in this area that are the most wind resistant, so are often stable enough to outlast storms and continue to grow through several iterations of a forest over a millennium. Still, many of the larger, centuries-old examples of these two species break off at their more fragile tops, and over time their centres fill with water and rot. They become unstable and prone to blowdown, and the timber inside slowly begins to lose its value. After decades as a timberman, Cronin could tell by looking at a tree's bark and the knots along its trunk if there was rot inside. The big Douglas fir held just the faintest twist in its trunk, which was free of limbs or blemishes up to its crown. When Cronin wrapped the green "LEAVE TREE" ribbon around its base, he secured it tightly with a knot.

Over the course of his career, Cronin had flagged other trees with green ribbon, but they were ones that he considered to hold non-merchantable wood: their trunks were too twisted or too flawed. When he laid eyes on the big Douglas fir in cutblock 7190, he could see immense timber value. "I'm a logger and I've taken out millions of trees. But I was impressed." He couldn't know with 100 percent certainty—"You don't know until you put a saw into it and by that point it's too late"—but the tree exhibited few of the telltale signs of rot or disease.

He had an encyclopedic knowledge of these forests, but could also see beyond a tree's rough bark to the dollar value of the timber within. "I can look at a tree and tell if it's got value or not. If it's not twisted, if the bark is healthy, if the limbs are healthy," Cronin said. "That one had value." Encased within the deeply crevassed bark of this Douglas fir lay enough wood to fill four logging trucks to capacity, with some to spare. If milled into dimensional lumber—two-by-fours, two-by-sixes, and the like—it could be used to frame five 2,000-square-foot houses. At first glance, he assessed the single tree in unprocessed log value at around $20,000. But since it was a Douglas fir, with its coveted warm colour and pronounced grain, the tree could be turned into higher-priced beams and posts for houses in Victoria and Vancouver. This single tree could fetch more than $50,000.

A site plan for the fallers had already been drawn, but at Cronin's insistence it was redone to take into account the Douglas fir he had flagged in the middle of the forest. It cost Teal Jones around $1,000 to redraw the site plans alone. In the middle of the map, Cronin and Van Hell dropped an icon the shape of a single tree, marking the location of the designated Douglas fir. The felling crew would be forced to honour this map: a single icon on a page, and a thin, tearable ribbon around a broad trunk—that would prove the strongest form of protection.

LESS THAN A YEAR after Cronin wrapped the green flagging around the big Douglas fir, the trees of cutblock 7190 were gone. Throughout the summer of 2011, the grove of old-growth forest stood awaiting its fate. When the October rains turned heavy, a sound erupted in the cool morning air: fallers, contracted by Teal Jones, were starting up their chainsaws. Following Dennis Cronin's ribbon markers and the map drawn by Walter Van Hell, the fallers began bringing down the trees. The teeth of the saws bit into half-a-millennium-old trunks, casting arcs of sawdust that settled over sword fern and moss. The cut conifer quickly filled the air with a thick, woodsy perfume. The giant cedars and firs hit the forest floor with thunderous thuds, but the trees might as well have made no sound at all.

A crew of hooktenders wrapped cables around the trunks of the fallen trees, attaching the lines to a cable yarder positioned on the road above the clear-cut. One by one the logs were hauled and loaded onto trucks, driven across the bridge over the Gordon River, past a group of anti-logging activists standing next to a grove of old-growth forest, and across the island to the town of Lake Cowichan, where Dennis Cronin lived. From there, the logs were trucked up-island to Nanaimo, where they were dropped into the ocean and incorporated into a boom. Tugboats hauled the boom across the Strait of Georgia, under the bridges of Vancouver, and up the Fraser River to the Teal Jones mill on the mainland. Unlike many logs that are exported whole, or raw, for processing and manufacturing, those of cutblock 7190 remained in the province. They were de-barked and run through a milling machine, which dissected them into timbers of various lengths and dimensions. There are beams of houses or pieces of furniture, windows or doorframes, guitars or works of art, that are made from the wood harvested from cutblock 7190.

After a few months, silence returned to the base of Edinburgh Mountain. The fallers had long since packed up their chainsaws and gear; the trucks, laden with logs, had departed. A faint dusting of snow fell onto the clear-cut. As spring came, any remaining mounds of moss and bushes of salal crackled and dried up in the unfiltered sun. Bears that had called this patch of forest home found other hollows to den, while birds sought other branches to roost. Every wiry cedar, every droopy-topped hemlock, and every great fir that once made up this rainforest grove was gone—every tree, except one.

Culturally modified trees, like this one found on Flores Island in Clayoquot Sound, Vancouver Island — where the anti-logging campaign known as the War in the Woods was sparked — are used by many First Nations in coastal British Columbia as records of their historical presence and forest use. (Photograph by Harley Rustad)

The controversial photograph of the Cary Fir, an allegedly 126.2-metre-tall Douglas fir said to be felled near Vancouver in 1895 by logger George Cary, has been widely accepted as a hoax. (Image C-06489 courtesy of the Royal BC Museum and Archives)

Timber workers for A And L Logging Co., circa 1926, using a large Douglas fir on Vancouver Island as a spar tree, an anchor point for cables pulled by a steam "donkey" to haul logs out of a cutblock. (Image D-04875 courtesy of the Royal BC Museum and Archives)

Logger Dennis Cronin beside the large Douglas fir in cutblock 7190 that would come to be named Big Lonely Doug — pictured here the day he wrapped the green "Leave Tree" flagging around its trunk. (Courtesy of Lorraine Cronin)

Big Lonely Doug surrounded by the clear-cut remains of cutblock 7190. Around the cutblock is the old-growth forest known as Eden Grove and the replanted second-growth forests in the Gordon River Valley, near Port Renfrew. (Photograph by TJ Watt)

Activist, photographer, and big tree hunter TJ Watt in Eden Grove, an intact patch of old-growth forest next door to Big Lonely Doug. (Photograph by Björn Hermannes)

A tree climber, part of a group of forest activists that accurately measured the height of Big Lonely Doug in May 2014, hauls himself towards the canopy of the second-largest Douglas fir in Canada. (Photograph by TJ Watt)

Ancient Forest Alliance founder Ken Wu alongside the stump of a western red cedar that was cut near Big Lonely Doug and that sparked the petition for formally protecting Avatar Grove. (Photograph by TJ Watt)

CHAPTER 8

Last Tree Standing

DENNIS CRONIN'S BIG DOUGLAS fir swayed quietly on its own in the middle of cutblock 7190. Winds swirled, grey mist rolled off the Pacific to fill the valley, and the sun rose and set. But the tree stood.

One morning, the sun rose behind Edinburgh Mountain, rays fragmenting through the trees that cap its ridge. In the valley below, near the mountain's base, a single tree stood in darkness. Across the Gordon River, sunlight hit the tops of the hills before slowly descending down the slopes. Then, after most of the hills across the river were warmed with an orange glow, the broken top of a towering tree in the middle of a clear-cut was illuminated, like the lighting of a solitary candle. The sun climbed higher above the mountain until the entire great Douglas fir was gradually revealed from under the mountain's shadow.

Along the rutted, principal logging road that ran through the Gordon River Valley, TJ Watt navigated his blue, right-side-drive Mitsubishi Delica, scanning the hills on either side through the windows. The tall van bumped this way and that, over a road that in parts had been packed smooth by heavy logging trucks laden with timber, while other areas were washed-out rough, as if paved with petrified loaves of bread. The hillsides in the Gordon River Valley were a patchwork quilt of cutblocks in various stages of regrowth. Some hills appeared cartoonish, as if drawn in a child's scribble book, with canopies of replanted saplings growing in unison to form a single layer. From a distance, the second growth looked less like forests than fields of even-aged wheat.

There were fresh cutblocks, too, with stumps and scraps of cedar and fir, bright orange and ochre as if still warm from the chainsaws and machines that had cut them down. There was little remaining in these patches—a few fragments and splinters left behind after the logs had been hauled away.

And there was old growth, when Watt looked closely, clinging to the very tops of a steep mountainside or down the plunging bottom of a gorge. These were the inaccessible trees, too far or too difficult or too costly to access by a timber company.

It was a cool day in February 2012 as Watt approached Avatar Grove. The forest he had helped protect was drawing tourists from afar. This time he kept going past the grove, farther into the spiderweb of dirt logging roads that covers much of the southern half of the Vancouver Island.

Watt had grown used to seeing trees disappear. In his role as campaigner and photographer for the Ancient Forest Alliance, he had driven thousands of kilometres of logging roads looking for the island's dwindling old-growth forests. Over the years, his expeditions to find groves untouched by commercial logging had forced him to delve deeper, along the rough backroads of the island, up mountainsides and down valleys, in search of Canada's last great trees.

More often than not, what Watt found was not intact forests but fresh clear-cuts. Driving along these roads felt like peering into a post-apocalyptic future: dry, dusty, barren—a wasteland of destruction. But every so often, at the end of a road, he found a glimpse of a glimmering and verdant past—a remnant of a forest that had been left largely undisturbed for millennia. When he spotted the telltale signs of large, ancient trees emerging from a canopy, he would park his vehicle alongside the dirt road and head into the tangled forest on foot. It was no easy job to traverse some of the densest forest ecosystems in Canada, where an hour can pass, and you've advanced only a couple hundred metres, where undergrowth forms impenetrable barriers of bracken and bush, and where wild animals of tooth and antler lurk. But possibility compelled him farther, up hill and over creek, in the hope of finding some of the largest trees in the world—placid leviathans waiting in the forest.

With each kilometre he drove and every ramble he took, the clock kept ticking. Logging companies continued to build new roads in a feverish bid to access new groves. Watt was trying to find them before a logger did. With each expedition into the bush, he could feel the race to locate, and hopefully protect, a small fraction of the province's arboreal legacy before it was permanently cut away. His goal was to bring back evidence not only that clear-cutting old growth continues to occur, but that there are still forests that can be saved from the saw.

If you aren't familiar with the roads and terrain here, it is easy to become lost. Take one wrong turn and you can drive for hours, switchbacking up and down hills before arriving at one of the thousands of dead ends that mark the extremes of a logging company's reach. But Watt was familiar with this area. He had explored the valley that follows the Gordon River dozens of times, and he knew where he was going: to a patch of forest at the base of Edinburgh Mountain that was part of one of the largest continuous unprotected tracts of old-growth forest on the island. Located alongside the river, on a gentle slope, it was a prime candidate for producing big trees.

Out the window to his right, something caught his eye: the unmistakable orange of a fresh clear-cut. He knew the road would lead to the stumps, to where he had been hoping to find trees. After turning onto a spur road he was forced to stop at a locked gate, a clear sign that there was current logging activity in the area. Watt grabbed his camera and continued on foot, across a single-lane wooden bridge. A hundred feet below, the emerald-green waters of the Gordon River thundered towards the Pacific Ocean a few kilometres away. On either side of the road grew young alders, often the first species to regrow after a cut. The area had seen much logging over the years, with replanted forests filling in the blanks.

Farther down the road, the smell of conifer grew stronger, of cut wood and glossy needles releasing their oils into the air. He rounded a bend, glanced to his right, and stopped. The patch of old growth he had come to hike through was gone—a bite had been taken out of the forest. It was a familiar feeling for Watt, to return to photograph a lush ancient forest only to find it levelled. If you make enough trips off the island's main roads, the excursions begin to feel like surprise funerals. Watt often returned home from a weekend to compare his photographs of a recent clear-cut with images he had taken only months previous. It was jarring to witness: before and after, green and grey.

Before him, this time, was a scene altogether different from any he had ever photographed. It wasn't a forest or a clear-cut; it wasn't an unblemished ecosystem or the scarred remains of an industrial harvest, but something he had never seen. What stood out to Watt wasn't the fact that yet another section of old-growth forest had been decimated, but that in the middle of the cutblock a single tree remained standing. It was a Douglas fir—and it was enormous. The tree was limbless from its base to 80 percent of its height, where a crooked crown of branches held dark green needles that ruffled gently in the breeze. One of the branches—which bent down and then up like a flexed arm—could have been a tree in and of itself. He brought his camera to his eye. Through the viewfinder, he framed an image unlike any he had taken before.

In the middle of the clear-cut, the giant fir stood like an obelisk in a desert.

FROM THE ROAD ABOVE the cutblock, the scene looked like the aftermath of a nuclear detonation: a blast of destruction that ended abruptly at the shockwave's farthest point. But at the centre was not a crater but a single tree. The clear-cut was fresh: branches that had been cut off from logs still held their green needles, and fractured remnants of hundreds of firs, cedars, and hemlocks had yet to turn from warm orange and yellow to sun-bleached grey. The clear-cut was scattered with trunks, branches, and shattered wood—anything deemed of little or no value to the timber company that had come and gone. An excavator had been left within the cutblock and a cable yarder on the slope above, where the clear-cutting extended across the road and up the hillside. Cut and branchless logs lay in haphazard piles, the scene like a game of pick-up-sticks abandoned by a giant.

A fresh cutblock is a jarring sight to behold. Along each colossal stump runs a ridge of splintered wood, marking as far as the chainsaw can enter the trunk and where the tree fractured as it fell. Emily Carr, in her wanderings of Vancouver Island in search of landscapes to paint, called these remains "screamers." They are "the cry of the tree's heart," she wrote, "wrenching and tearing apart just before she gives that sway and the dreadful groan of falling, that dreadful pause while her executioners step back with their saws and axes resting and watch. It's a horrible sight to see a tree felled, even now, though the stumps are grey and rotting. As you pass among them you see their screamers sticking up out of their own tombstones, as it were. They are their own tombstones and their own mourners."

This was part of what the Ancient Forest Alliance was calling the Christy Clark Grove, the campaign that wasn't resonating with the public like Avatar Grove. The reality was settling upon TJ Watt. He had driven along this very logging road many times in the previous two years. He had crossed the bridge high above the Gordon River, followed the bumpy track flanked by second growth, and driven between two towering groves of old growth at the base of Edinburgh Mountain. He had passed cedars and Douglas firs that flanked the road as if he were driving between skyscrapers of a downtown core. He had hiked down into the old growth, taking pictures of any big tree he came across. If he had only crossed a small creek and continued through the bush for a hundred metres or so, he would have found himself standing under the second-largest Douglas fir in the country.

Or he might have walked close but never seen it, as he focused on not breaking an ankle in a crevasse made by moss and root, or as he trudged around impenetrable barriers of undergrowth and deadfall. He could have been within a few dozen metres of such a gargantuan tree and walked right past it—the forest forcing him to follow its own paths, which may lead to danger or discovery. Watt had been so close, and yet he might as well have been another valley away.

As he stared across the ruin of a forest, a familiar feeling of frustration and anger set in—at the logging company for harvesting yet another old-growth grove, and at himself for not identifying it or protecting it in time. But he could only do so much. The rate at which forests were being cut far exceeded the ground a few eager activists could cover.

Dispirited, Watt continued down the road to hike in the adjacent grove of intact old growth. He wanted to feel the soft, spongy earth under his boots, smell the conifers and peat, and hear the creeks babbling between the trees. He wanted the comfort of being in an intact forest.

When Watt returned to Victoria, he mentioned the clear-cut with the solitary big tree to Ken Wu. But with the campaign to protect Avatar Grove reaching its climax, and an announcement imminent, it was shrugged off. Wu knew that timber workers sometimes leave individual trees or patches of trees, so it didn't sound that unusual. All attention was on developing Avatar into a premier tourist destination.

A month later, while accompanying a documentary-filmmaking student who was interested in filming clear-cuts, Watt finally descended into cutblock 7190 to stand under the towering Douglas fir, which stood on a flat plateau at the bottom of a slope. Dried twigs and slash snapped loudly under his boots. He scrambled over the jumble of deadwood and past three-metre-wide cedar stumps. He tiptoed along what had once been a nurse log, now scrubbed of the miniature forest of seedlings that had been growing along its length. With every step farther down into the clear-cut, the tree kept getting bigger and bigger and bigger until it towered above him, blocking out the sun.

TJ Watt looked up. In that moment, he knew he had stumbled upon something significant. To his eye, as someone who had spent years documenting Vancouver Island's big trees, this fir looked to be one of the largest in Canada. He had visited the largest known Douglas fir in the world many times—the Red Creek Fir, a giant 73.8 metres tall and 4.2 metres in diameter, located an hour away down several twisty turns of logging road. This one appeared roughly the same size.

Watt's initial photographs of the tree had no point of reference, and without a forest to compare it to, no scale. But this time, Watt returned to Ken Wu with a photograph of him standing on a cut hemlock stump adjacent to the enormous Douglas fir, leaning in and touching the tree's broad trunk. The photograph sent tingles down Wu's spine. The scale was key. Seeing a human dwarfed by the tree made all the difference.

Wu had to see it for himself.

"This could be the biggest Douglas fir in the country!" Wu said to Watt, after the pair made the trip to Port Renfrew to stand in the middle of cutblock 7190 and look up at the solitary tree. In that moment, the two activists realized that this tree presented a different opportunity than an intact old-growth forest.

The pair stumbled around the cutblock. Among the discarded branches were the stumps of once-ancient cedars and firs. Wu and Watt climbed on top to examine each one's rings. Some trees, they estimated, had been around five hundred years old.

It is a challenge for any environmental activist to motivate the public into action—to write to a politician, to join a protest, or simply to vote in an election with an issue such as old-growth protection in mind. For Wu, activists need something for the public to rally around: a point of tension, a symbol, an icon. The general concept of protecting old growth can never resonate as much as a place that people can walk through, touch, and see.

Environmental photographers can help bring what is often a remote issue into the home. But images of a babbling creek surrounded by forest, of a bear being dwarfed by a tree, of an eagle soaring over a valley, these all tend to blend together. They can be beautiful, but they are rarely effective. The challenge, for an activist pushing a cause, is to find an image—a symbol—that transcends nature and starts making people think.

There, in the middle of cutblock 7190, stood something different. Hope amid devastation. Life enduring against the odds. This tree provided exactly what the Ancient Forest Alliance needed: an image that symbolized its cause. What TJ Watt hadn't fully recognized on his first visit now became clear: this was an opportunity.

CHAPTER 9

Growing an Icon

ON MARCH 21, 2014 — timed to the International Day of Forests — the Ancient Forest Alliance issued a press release titled "Canada's Most Significant Big Tree Discovery in Decades!" Attached was the self-portrait of TJ Watt leaning against the tree, and the claim that it was possibly the second-largest Douglas fir in the country, just behind the Red Creek Fir, measured by calculating its total volume.

The tree was perfect. It was a near record-breaker. It was close to Port Renfrew, a town humming with activity around big-tree tourism after Avatar Grove. And it was alone. It was a site that could be visited by tourists, whose photographs wouldn't even need a caption. The tree summarized the entirety of the AFA's old-growth forest conservation issue in a single staggering blink. The Ancient Forest Alliance gave it a name: Big Lonely Doug.

"The days of colossal trees like these are quickly coming to an end as the timber industry cherry-picks the last unprotected, valley-bottom, lower-elevation ancient stands in southern B.C. where giants like this grow," Ken Wu stated in the release.

"It's time for the B.C. government to stop being more enthusiastic about big stumps than big trees, and for them to enact forest policies that protect our last endangered ancient forest ecosystems," TJ Watt noted, hoping this single tree might push a change in legislation.

Big Lonely Doug instantly became a celebrity. This wasn't just any tree in a forest. This was a sole survivor standing amid ruin. And its anthropomorphization resonated with people. It had a name, and a sad one, too. The press release remarked that the tree's trunk bore a scar in its bark around the base. Throughout Vancouver Island's logging history, large Douglas firs have often been used for their strength and stability as an aid in hauling felled logs from a cutblock. A crew might wrap cables around a prominent trunk to use it as an anchor for hauling logs. The cable would dig into the thick bark of the tree as a steam donkey or machine hauled.

The scar around the base of Big Lonely Doug wasn't there when Dennis Cronin wrapped green ribbon around its trunk. If the tree had been used as a yarding point by the hauling crew of cutblock 7190, that wasn't his intention.

But the logging crew saw strength in the tree's size and girth that could be employed. As its first act as a solitary tree, it was turned into a spar to haul logs from the cutblock. The image of the tree presented by the AFA was not only that of a survivor but a victim—forced to bear witness to the razing of its forest, while simultaneously being used as an aid in its destruction. The story rippled through the media, with the *Globe and Mail* calling the tree "sad" and "perhaps the loneliest tree in Canada."

Many timber workers, including some of Dennis Cronin's co-workers, met the media attention with little more than eye rolls. Fallers and forest engineers immediately questioned the "second-largest Douglas fir" designation given to Big Lonely Doug. To many people in the industry, "tallest," "largest," "widest," and perhaps especially "gnarliest" are little more than monikers that help promote an activist cause and attract attention—just another way of commercializing the trees. Activists may not sell the timber, but they sell the trees.

During more than a century of commercial logging on Vancouver Island, timber workers have encountered hundreds if not thousands of trees larger than

Big Lonely Doug. Nearly every single one has come down. Mike Pegg, who worked with Cronin at Teal Jones, noted another Douglas fir, just off a spur road and up a hillside nearby in the Gordon River Valley. He said it was bigger than Big Lonely Doug. But the tree had been blown over by the wind. There have existed much wider and taller Douglas firs, but apart from a handful, including the Red Creek Fir, none of them are still standing. They've been felled by chainsaw or axe, or have succumbed to a vicious storm. Regardless of their size, they have fallen. A tree cannot be a record holder if it no longer exists. The oldest person in the world does not retain her crown when she dies.

The difference is one of perspective: to those in the industry, a record tree is a record tree, regardless of whether it is alive and standing or fallen and dead. But to activists and ecologists, the value in these trees isn't finite. The return on these forests doesn't have to end when the wall of a house is erected.

As soon as Big Lonely Doug hit the media, questions began to surface about its survival. Amid the wonder and awe at such an unusual sight was concern for the tree now that its forest buffer had been cut. "The fact that all of the surrounding old-growth trees have been clear-cut around such a globally exceptional tree, putting it at risk of being damaged or blown down by windstorms, underscores the urgency for new provincial laws to protect B.C.'s largest trees, monumental groves, and endangered old-growth ecosystems," Ken Wu said in the press release.

"Lonely Doug is far more susceptible to blow-down in a serious wind now that his forest mates are gone. There's a metaphor there for us on the planet," one commenter posted under a news article about the tree.

"If there is a major storm in summer or winter, sadly this great tree that has seen history could keel over," another wrote.

These gargantuan trees, despite having endured for centuries, do fall. On New Year's Day 1997, a fierce windstorm tore through MacMillan Provincial Park, home to Cathedral Grove—a stand of easily accessible ancient Douglas firs situated alongside the narrow cross-island highway to Tofino. The wind knocked down some of the grove's largest trees and reshaped the structure of the park. In 2003, a sixty-metre-tall Douglas fir in Cathedral Grove came crashing down onto a parked car, killing two people inside.

Along the Koksilah River, less than an hour's drive north of Victoria, stood a Douglas fir that had been left by timber workers who proceeded to cut most of the surrounding forest. The seven-hundred-year-old tree blew down in a storm in 1979 because, ecologists asserted, it was without its protective buffer. At nearly four metres in diameter, the Koksilah Tree was one of the largest Douglas firs ever documented, and at the time held the record of being the second-largest Douglas fir in Canada, at 69.2 metres tall. Its fallen log became incorporated into a nature trail where hikers could walk along its length, gripping the furrowed bark of a ruined tower of old growth with their boots. Many activists point to the Koksilah Tree as an example of why saving individual trees—whether by activists or by loggers—is a more short-sighted approach to protecting old growth.

The projection that Big Lonely Doug would suffer the same fate appeared on the surface to make logical sense, but it overlooked several less-obvious ecological forces at work. Storms off the Pacific Ocean have hammered southern Vancouver Island for millennia. One sudden and riotous wind can be found just up the coast from Port Renfrew, where high pressure on the west side of the island forces wind through the Alberni Valley and across the entire island. The system is known as a Qualicum, after the beach and surf town on the island's eastern coast where the wind disgorges into the Strait of Georgia. But ferocious winds are known to race up every valley that runs perpendicular to the Pacific, battering the trees that stand dozens of kilometres from the coast. Over time, this strength training creates robust root systems, and while branches may occasionally blow off, those trees that endure grow thicker with each passing storm. Wind also acts as a form of brute natural selection, picking off the weaker and older trees with rot in their centres, or those that never had strong root systems to begin with. Wind is a relentless force along the coast, and if a tree cannot withstand the torture, it falls. Those that can, survive.

Many of the large trees that have fallen in storms have blown down not because of exposure but because of age. While these giants may seem to be god-like eternal beings that have survived a thousand years, and should therefore survive a thousand more, they are impermanent, with an inevitable death—just like anything crawling or growing or lurking in a forest, regardless of size or stature.

Big Lonely Doug had endured strong winds for as long as its latest apple-green needles protruded above the forest canopy. Before cutblock 7190 was felled, the tree's crown stood well above the treetops, where it bore the full brunt of winds that coursed through the valley every year. The tree bears several scars from the wind that predate the loss of its forest buffer, including a broken top—as many of the largest Douglas firs do—like the chipped turret of a castle constantly under siege.

When Dennis Cronin first walked the stand, among the dozen or so exceptionally large cedars and firs he noticed something unusual about this particular patch of forest: there was a significant gap in the age range between the largest trees—some three metres wide—and the rest of the grove. There was a collection of large cedar and fir stumps, around or greater than five hundred years old, but the majority of the stumps were from hemlocks of about one hundred years old. To an experienced forester, it was a clear sign that the majority of the forest had grown back after some kind of hurricane-force gale had torn through the valley and knocked down the weaker and less-established trees. The great trees, including Big Lonely Doug, withstood the storm.

"Ninety-nine percent of that forest would've been flattened right at the turn of the century," Cronin said. He could see it in the forest as clearly as seeing grandparents among a group of children. "But that tree," he added, referring to the Douglas fir he had flagged, "it probably lived through four or five rotations of the forest in the time that it was alive."

When forest ecologist Andy MacKinnon saw a picture of Big Lonely Doug, his first thought was that the tree would not remain standing for long with its companions gone and its location in a notoriously windy place. But when he visited the cutblock, he noticed a pattern in the age range as Cronin had, and one that he could measure in the rings of the remaining stumps.

What both men observed, before and after the clearcut, was that a cataclysmic storm had ripped across southern Vancouver Island perhaps a century ago. It was a storm that the Pacheedaht remembered, that ecologists could see evidence of in the forest, and that Teal Jones had noted on its maps when estimating the dominant age of the stand. But the specifics—the first-hand written account—had long been forgotten.

In 1906, the Victoria-based timber operator H. H. Jones was hired by a businessman out of Minneapolis named T. W. Welter to locate some fine timber on southern Vancouver Island. Welter was one of many Americans who saw untapped wealth within the forests of British Columbia and began cruising for land claims. Jones knew of some stands of big timber that lay on the way to the headwaters of the Gordon River, most easily accessible at that time via the interior of the island rather than the coast. He enlisted one of Welter's timber cruisers, a man named John McClure, who would assess the value of the trees for his boss, and formed a group with an Indigenous man named Fred who they met in Duncan and a Swedish man named Henry.

After days of trekking through the forest with their gear, the foursome made camp along the Gordon River and set about surveying the timber. Before crawling into their tent for the night, they laid out "forty-five sections of as fine timber as every grew," as H. H. Jones wrote in "A Cyclone Among the Timber Titans," an article for a 1911 issue of *British Columbia Magazine*. As darkness fell, the weather turned.

> The air was still; in fact, there was no sound, save the cry of a timber wolf or the thud of a lump of soft snow dropping from its perch high in the tree-tops to the earth beneath, breaking the silence. But a storm was coming in from the Pacific—a storm without a precedent in the centuries in which those gigantic specimens of forest trees had made their growth, and one not likely to be repeated for centuries to come. A runaway from its natural course was upon us. It had no introduction—and certainly required none. I have been in some very bad storms; have seen houses swing from their foundation, roofs removed, trees shattered, and have witnessed the death of both man and beast during terrible storms, but I never knew of one which had not given some warning of its approach.

The timber workers were stuck, precariously situated with little more than a canvas tent as protection, as trees crashed to the earth around them. The trunks hit the ground like blasts of dynamite, which Jones likened to the shocking spontaneity of a fireworks display. In three gargantuan waves the storm hammered the forest, until finally it subsided. When the same storm passed south over Washington State, it claimed the lives of three men who were killed when a tree fell on their shack.

"It would be equally difficult to estimate the velocity of the fiend which laid waste so much wealth in its mad frolic," Jones wrote. "Had it struck the wind gauge at the meteorological office, it certainly would have heated the bearing of that instrument."

In the morning, Jones and his companions rushed outside to assess the destruction.

> The storm, on a line from west to east, running within ten feet of our tent, had cut every tree and left them piled in a tangled mass in places fifty feet high. They were not uprooted, but broken off from ten to thirty feet above the ground. Trees from three to five feet in diameter were smashed as if but twigs. The mighty rush of the storm allowed no chance for the forest giants to sway and loosen their roots. They were pushed forward with one mighty strain until they broke.

But the storm had not destroyed every tree. Some of the oldest and largest trees—western red cedars with broad bases, Douglas firs with deep roots, and Sitka spruces with columnar trunks—remained.

Dennis Cronin and Andy MacKinnon, from their two perspectives as forest engineer and ecologist respectively, had found evidence in the Gordon River Valley of a legendary great wind that tore across southern Vancouver Island—in some places devastating entire forests. After taking into account the forest's ecological history, and walking the cutblock himself, MacKinnon quickly changed his perspective on Big Lonely Doug's situation—it was not as bleak as he had originally thought.

Cronin never had doubts about the stability of such a healthy, substantial Douglas fir that had withstood storm after storm battering its branches. "He's used to the wind," he said, "so he's got a chance."

Further evidence of Big Lonely Doug's survival can be found even further back in the dendrochronology of this particular patch of the Gordon River Valley. The tree is estimated to be approximately a thousand years old, but the stumps of the next-oldest trees in the cutblock were dated to around five hundred years. The evidence suggests that these trees—around a dozen western red cedars and Douglas firs—sprouted through the wreckage of another hurricane-force storm, that lashed the region half a millennium ago. But amid the ruin, one tree had survived.

It wasn't the only time the tree that would be known as Big Lonely Doug would stand alone.

IN THE SPRING OF 2014, Dennis Cronin was at home watching TV when a news program came on. The screen flashed with an image of the misty hills of the Gordon River Valley that he knew so well, of a clear-cut, and of a single enormous Douglas fir towering above someone standing at its base. He started laughing and called his wife, Lorraine, into the room.

"There's my tree!" the logger exclaimed.

He was shocked but not surprised. After cutblock 7190 was harvested, he had returned to the tree and noticed bootprints in the mud around its base—possibly from wood salvagers but more likely from activists. It was only a matter of time, he'd thought, that the tree would be found by an organization like the Ancient Forest Alliance.

On screen came TJ Watt and Ken Wu, talking about the last remaining old-growth forests in the region. Wu pointed to a large branch, nearly a foot thick, lying on the ground at the base of the Douglas fir, saying that it had been ripped off of Big Lonely Doug by a recent storm due to the loss of its forest buffer.

"And potentially the tree itself could be blown down," Wu said as he was being interviewed near the tree.

"To lose Big Lonely Doug would be a tragedy," Watt reiterated in the news clip. "It's a sad enough scene as it already is."

It was a claim that struck Cronin as he watched. The excitement over seeing the tree he'd saved on TV soon turned to resentment. He was one of the few people to have walked the forest before it was cut and knew that particular tree had grown well above the canopy, feeling the full brunt of winds against its branches for centuries. To him, the claim that it was now more vulnerable was just another example of activist "doom and gloom-ers" using "scare tactics," as he put it, to galvanize the public into action. Trees lose branches every blustery season or succumb to the wind entirely, even when they are standing in an intact forest. The broken branch lying at Big Lonely Doug's base was not a consequence of loggers isolating this one tree, Cronin maintained, but simply an occurrence within the natural cycle of these forests.

He had met many environmental activist groups over the years. Like other timber workers—fallers, truck drivers, engineers—he would pass them in his truck on his way to a cutblock while they were out looking for old growth. Maybe they would exchange a wave; maybe not. Still, Cronin had a job to do, and that job, at least superficially, was at odds with what the activists were trying to achieve. He disagreed with many of their tactics, remembering the fear he'd felt when working in the Carmanah region during the early 1990s and the worry that someone he knew, one of his co-workers and friends, might hit a spiked tree with their chainsaw and be seriously hurt or even killed. Elsewhere, including in the Walbran Valley, he had come across activists having tampered with the loggers' work by painting over their spray paint with brown in an attempt to camouflage the markings. Or they would remove the brightly coloured flagging tape—sometimes even retying the pink "ROAD LOCATION" tape to branches that would steer timber workers down an errant path through the forest, eventually leading to the edge of a cliff. There was little Cronin could do amid an increasingly negative climate that was turning loggers into villains. He would just keep working.

Cronin had figured he would hear about the big fir in cutblock 7190 eventually, just not it being presented as a new "discovery" of an organization ostensibly at odds with his work. It was he who had wrapped the green ribbon around its base and pushed his bosses to set it aside. Without him, the Douglas fir would be planks and boards and beams. Lorraine was keen to set the record straight, and emailed the Ancient Forest Alliance to let them know that the tree wouldn't be standing if not for her husband—a logger.

But it was too late: Big Lonely Doug had become an unwitting mascot for an environmental cause.

CHAPTER 10

Big Tree Hunting

FOR THOUSANDS OF YEARS the residents of Vancouver Island have hunted big timber. It began with the coastal First Nations, who sought out large cedars deep in the forests, carefully selecting ideal specimens of western red cedar from which to carve their canoes. Then, Scottish botanists headed into uncharted bush with notebook and pencil to track down, document, and collect samples of some of the biggest trees in the world. Next, as the forest became a commercial resource, settlers delved deeper into the island's heart to locate the highest-value stands and brilliantly engineered how to extract the mammoth trees. And when environmental activists of the 1980s and '90s began to realize the scope of what was being logged — and of what remained—they found immense groves, like those in Carmanah and Clayoquot, and singular specimens to be at the centre of their campaigns. Now, tourists are going off the well-trodden paths to find the latest record-breaking tree.

In the mid-1980s, as eyes began falling on valuable regions of old-growth forest on Vancouver Island such as Carmanah and Clayoquot and Walbran, the question of how much remained arose. After decades of timber harvesting, there was no universally accepted record of forest untouched by commercial logging, nor of remaining big trees. The most comprehensive archive had been casually collected by Randy Stoltmann, the activist who had first alerted the threat of logging Carmanah and who first began documenting the large trees around his home as a high school student in West Vancouver. By the age of twenty-four, he had personally visited, searched out, and collected information on many of the remaining significant trees in British Columbia.

Stoltmann's records and notes formed the foundation of the province's first prominent inventory in 1986, in partnership with the B.C. Forestry Association. The B.C. BigTree Registry's goal was to encourage outdoor and environmental enthusiasts to locate, describe, and catalogue the largest trees of each species "to produce an official register, and to provide protection for these special trees," read a WCWC pamphlet, and to mail in their findings. But on May 21, 1994, Stoltmann died in an avalanche while ski-mountaineering. Recognizing his efforts to protect the Carmanah Valley, the provincial government renamed Heaven Grove, the patch of Sitka spruces once the location of Camp Heaven in Carmanah Walbran Provincial Park, the "Randy Stoltmann Commemorative Grove." At Stoltmann's funeral, his friend and fellow activist Clinton Webb, who had been with Stoltmann the day the pair stumbled upon evidence that MacMillan Bloedel was moving towards logging Carmanah, concluded his eulogy: "Let us make sure that in the falling of a great tree to the earth, the hole in the forest canopy is soon filled with the vigorous growth of many saplings."

After Stoltmann's sudden death, the B.C. BigTree Registry fell from priority, and some of his handwritten records, research, and maps went missing. Some, however, he had copied into a report for the B.C. Conservation Data Centre, which was passed to the Ministry of Forests and Range, and then, in 2010, to the University of British Columbia's faculty of forestry. In October 2014, seven months after Big Lonely Doug was presented to the public by the Ancient Forest Alliance, the registry was launched online, becoming a searchable database of record for the province's largest, tallest, and widest trees. True to its original ethos, the registry remains open to the public for additions.

Newly identified trees can be submitted online with measurements, descriptions, and photographs, which are assessed, confirmed, and added to the registry.

Trees that make it to the registry are approved based on certain superlatives—tallest, largest base circumference, or largest in total volume—and ordered in top-ten lists. Using a method devised by an American forester named Fred Besley in 1925, each tree is awarded a score based on tree height, circumference, and crown spread, with the greatest appointed a "champion." Vancouver Island and the Gulf Islands boast eight champions. The largest shore pine grows in Esquimalt, just outside Victoria, and the largest Pacific dogwood flowers every spring on Salt Spring Island. But the forests around Port Renfrew hold the region's most impressive trees. An hour east of town, down several twists and turns of logging roads flanked by clear-cuts, grows the Red Creek Fir, the world's largest Douglas fir. The Cheewhat Giant grows off the logging road to Carmanah Walbran Provincial Park, and is the largest western red cedar as well as the largest tree by volume in the country. And the Carmanah Giant, not only Canada's tallest Sitka spruce but also the country's tallest tree at more than ninety-five metres, grows just up the coast from Port Renfrew.

Many of the province's most significant trees are growing on Crown land—and possibly available to timber companies to cut. They were also likely found and nominated to the BigTree Registry by activists, environmentalists, or people who have an interest in protecting the trees and the forests. Since its inception, the registry has meant not just to be a record but also a tool for conservation. For a tree like Big Lonely Doug, its "second-largest Douglas fir in Canada" moniker is only true as long it remains undisputed. In all likelihood, at the bottom of a valley just beyond the furthest logging road's reach lies a record-breaking tree somewhere on southern Vancouver Island: a Douglas fir with a total size greater than the Red Creek Fir, a Sitka spruce even taller than the Carmanah Giant, or a western red cedar with a gnarly and twisted base even wider than any tree already identified. The wind is tickling their fragile tops while mist enshrouds their trunks. There may be record-breakers that reshape our understanding of their growth and their role in the forest. They may have been passed by Indigenous peoples many times over, but they have yet to be assessed with an eye for either commercial logging or large-scale protection.

For TJ Watt, the possibility of finding more giant trees spurs him on—to drive to the very end of a rocky logging road and continue on farther into the bush on foot. He has identified many; he could identify more. But Watt recognizes that the people who spend the most time in the remotest forests of the island aren't activists; they're loggers: "Often the first and last people who are seeing these forests are the people who are cutting them down." But for Watt, it doesn't have to be.

To find a giant is one step, to recognize its rarity and ecological value is another. But to turn the trees themselves into destinations would offer the greatest return; it would not only excite the new generation of environmentalists but would turn tourists into activists, hikers into big-tree hunters.

TWO MONTHS AFTER THE Ancient Forest Alliance introduced Big Lonely Doug to the world, TJ Watt stepped into a climbing harness on a sunny spring day, buckled a blue helmet under his chin, slung the strap of his bulky DSLR camera over his shoulder, and looked up. Cotton balls of white cloud rolled across a blue sky. He was about to climb one of the largest trees in the country.

Watt clipped into an ascender—a mechanism used to facilitate climbing by gripping and locking onto a rope—slipped his foot into a sling, and hauled himself up off the ground. Inch by inch, he slowly but surely ascended. The apparatus and technique were meant to summit a mountain, but were ideal for climbing a tree. The high-rig loggers of old would have used spiked boots and a sling wrapped around a tree to shimmy their way to the top, but the ascender allowed for the barest minimum of impact upon the tree.

Up Watt went. From a distance, he was a spider climbing a thread of silk beside a telephone pole. The wide trunk blocked out the sun like the moon in a solar eclipse. Even as he neared the crown of branches, despite tapering slightly the trunk still loomed beside him. The bark was close enough to touch.

It took Watt around fifteen minutes of hard work to reach the first branches. There, inside the canopy, he met Matthew Beatty—a co-founder of the Arboreal Collective, an informal network of like-minded professional arborists who advocate for the protection of old-growth forests through climbing big trees. The collective was one of several that had emerged in British Columbia, Washington, and Oregon—with names like Expedition Old Growth and Ascending the Giants—that aimed to add big-tree climbing to the roster of adventure tourism. To these tree climbers, seeking out and climbing the largest western red cedars, Sitka spruces, and Douglas firs on Canada's West Coast and in the United States' Pacific Northwest is to experience nature in a more intimate way. There lies great tourism potential, Beatty has seen—to bring people typically disconnected with the wilderness, these trees, and the issues surrounding the protection of old-growth forests into the treetops. It isn't standing at the base of a mountain looking up, but at the top of a mountain looking down.

There exists a deep history of activists around the world using sit-ins in trees as a protest tool. In 1971, in what was known as the Elm Conflict, people in Stockholm, Sweden, climbed into the treetops of several urban elms to protest the proposition to cut them down to make way for a subway expansion. In 1985, an activist named Mikal Jakubal climbed a Douglas fir in Oregon's Willamette National Forest to protest clear-cutting—sparking a series of similar tree sit-ins along the U.S. coast. The longest and most notorious was by Julia "Butterfly" Hill who, beginning in 1997, spent 738 days in the tops of a fifty-five-metre-tall coast redwood in California to save it from being felled. Her action led to the timber company placing the estimated 1,500-year-old tree, named Luna, and a buffer of forest around it off limits to logging.

Matthew Beatty sees tree climbing organizations in small part as an extension of that activist ethos, but more about connecting the public with these trees emotionally.

Beatty had brought his team of experienced tree climbers to Port Renfrew to climb Big Lonely Doug, to accurately measure its height and to create a promotional package of video and photography of the tree for the Ancient Forest Alliance. For Beatty, there was urgency to climb such an unusual tree as well. He, too, worried that Big Lonely Doug's isolated existence might not last long, that its lack of forest buffer would eventually prove fatal for the tree. Standing at the base, Beatty had pulled hard on a high-powered slingshot and let it fly. A beanbag attached to a thin line sailed more than fifty metres up and over one of Big Lonely Doug's thick branches. Using the line, he had hauled up a climbing rope and set the rigging to climb the tree. Taking care to minimize impact on the tree itself, the tree climbers employed a stationary rope system, where one end is anchored to avoid friction on the branch.

A woodpecker landed on one of the tree's limbs, before flittering off confused by the newcomers in the treetops. Beatty and Watt hung suspended among the branches. The two could see the entire valley. They could see the old-growth trees of Eden Grove, and the other cutblock flagged by Dennis Cronin and Walter Van Hell. They could see patches of replanted second growth, light green and verdant and uniform, around the valley.

Dozens of storeys in the air, even the light breeze caused the tree to sway side to side; they could feel the tree twist as it moved. Big Lonely Doug trembled as the valley stirred, but the breeze was a mere whisper of the great winds that had once knocked down the entire forest, leaving only a few aged giants behind.

Watt snapped photographs of small ferns and young honeysuckle bushes growing out of a moss-covered branch. But the ferns looked crinkled and dry without the moisture emanating from a rainforest below. He turned his camera down, to take the kind of photograph that he often uploaded to his website and Instagram page. Below him, there was only one thing that caught a shadow. Stretching across cutblock 7190 to nearly touch the patch of dark green old-growth forest next door was a long silhouette of a giant tree—like the shadow of a great sundial ticking and ticking around the clear-cut.

After months of speculation, Watt would finally have confirmation of the height of Big Lonely Doug. He had watched as another tree climber ascended higher through the canopy to reach the fractured tip that had broken off years, maybe decades, before. Only a twisted burl remained—bleached grey in the sun. Still, a few small huckleberries had sprouted in the fold of deadwood. Even at the pinnacle of the tree, twenty storeys above ground, death had fostered life.

The climber had shimmied his way up to the very top, steadied himself, and dropped a yellow measuring tape down alongside the trunk. Big Lonely Doug's height—from the tree's point of germination several metres under the mound of needles and shed bark up to its broken top—was confirmed at sixty-six metres tall, just shy of Dennis Cronin's estimation with his hypsometer the day he flagged the tree.

Climbing a skyscraper-sized tree requires some technical skill and experience, but the method to accurately measure its height is straightforward. Determining age, however, is a more challenging task. Dendrochronology, the study of a tree's age based on its growth rings, can be accurate to the year. Much can be learned by examining the rings of a tree—primarily any major environmental events that affected the tree's growth. A temperate and wet year during which the tree grew rapidly will form a thicker ring, while a drier year with more extreme seasons will produce a thinner ring. The appearance of thin lines on a stump or cut log are in reality variations in density and colour that form the tree's distinctive and countable rings.

To age a living, standing tree, however, is much more difficult. Using a technique called "core sampling," dendrochronologists employ a drill that bores into a trunk to harmlessly remove a pencil-thin column of the tree's core. This method was used to date what for decades was thought to be the oldest known tree, determined to be nearly five thousand years old. It sprouted through the earth around the same time as the bricks of the Great Pyramid of Egypt were being methodically stacked. The bristlecone pine, nicknamed Methuselah, grows somewhere within Inyo National

Forest, California, but its exact location has never been made public out of concern that it might be assaulted by trophy hunters keen on pilfering a branch of the ultimate record-breaker. It's a legitimate fear: in 1964, a dendrochronologist graduate student cut down the oldest known tree at the time, named Prometheus and also a bristlecone pine, when reportedly his core sampling bit failed. He determined the tree's age by killing it. In 2013, another example of the species was assessed to be older than Methuselah—more than five thousand years old—earning the crown as the oldest known tree in the world. The tree has yet to be given a name. These trees grow slowly in the harsh, high-elevation mountains, which is reflected in their dwarfed size compared to the great towers growing in the lush valleys of the Pacific temperate rainforests. For trees like Big Lonely Doug, with its nearly four-metre diameter, this method of dating is simply not possible; no bit is long enough to core through its enormous girth.

When Watt first stumbled upon Big Lonely Doug, he and several ecologists estimated the tree to be approximately a thousand years old, after comparing its width to the stumps of five-hundred- and six-hundred-year-old Douglas firs nearby. It would have been a seedling around the time the Viking Leif Erikson first landed on the east coast of North America and began building sod houses at L'Anse aux Meadows in what is now

Newfoundland. It would predate the formation of Canada by seven times. It would have been seven hundred years old, already a titan of the forest, when the great flood of 1700 surged along the coast.

Dennis Cronin had stood on more stumps than most, after decades working in the timber industry. He knew that on a rich, well-draining plateau in the lee of a mountain, Douglas firs grow well beyond how they would on a rockier, more arid slope. He maintained that the tree could easily prove to be more than a thousand years old. But until the tree falls—blown over by the wind when it finally becomes too old to repel the storms—how many times its shadow has been cast across the land will remain a mystery. Only with the fall of a giant will its impact really become known. Only death will reveal how long Big Lonely Doug has lived.

The image of a single surviving giant tree standing in the middle of a clear-cut began drawing tourists away from the beaches and hiking trails along the famed West Coast, and into logging country at the heart of Vancouver Island. Big Lonely Doug captivated people not because of a catchy cultural reference but because it held emotion. Visitors began asking at Port Renfrew's tourist-office-cum-community-centre for directions to the tree, wanting to "keep him company." People would go to hug the tree. They would go to sit underneath its canopy and look across the empty clear-cut. They would go to scramble over the scraps of forest for a picture where they appear the size of an ant.

The tree, and its name, had become the Ancient Forest Alliance's new Avatar Grove—the hook that drove attention to the organization and to the cause. To attract donations, the AFA began an Adopt-an-Ancient-Tree program, in which supporters could choose between eight individual trees—including the Red Creek Fir, the Cheewhat Giant, and Canada's Gnarliest Tree—or six groves and pay a minimum fifty dollars. Anyone who selects Big Lonely Doug, the campaign's spokesperson, receive a dedicated colour certificate marking him or her as "an adoptive guardian of Canada's 2nd largest Douglas fir tree, Big Lonely Doug" and someone "helping to support the Ancient Forest Alliance's campaign to protect British Columbia's endangered old-growth forests." The certificate is printed with a photo of the giant tree standing "lonely as ever" in a clear-cut. More generous donors are bestowed with a title: "Ancient Forest Defender" ($100) or "Ancient Forest Protector" ($200). It was a tried-and-tested marketing tactic by environmental non-profit and for-profit organizations to encourage participation in a cause. The World Wildlife Fund has been offering a similar "adoption" program for decades, where the donor receives a plush stuffed animal—a panda, a snow leopard, an orca—in return for their contribution.

Big Lonely Doug also lies in the ideal location for tree-hunting visitors who don't want to drive for hours through a warren of logging roads or trek for kilometres through thick bush to take in the sight. And the tree stands far enough off the main paved road that finding it feels like an adventure—a mini-expedition just off the beaten track. It feels like a search for an endangered beast that was thought to have died out long ago. When the tree comes into view, there is as much relief as there is awe: Big Lonely Doug is still there. It is still standing.

Big Lonely Doug began to appear in the marketing campaigns of a variety of organizations and companies. Expectedly, numerous environmental advocacy groups used photographs of the tree to elicit donations. Businesses saw value in the tree as well. Sitka, a Victoria-based clothing company, started a funding campaign to raise money to improve the trail through the cutblock and construct a viewing platform around the tree to protect its roots, "now that people are coming to visit Big Lonely Doug to keep him company." They used a photo of the tree in the clear-cut, writing, "Doug is lonely because his old-growth friends were clear-cut all around him in 2012." The campaign also helped raise $4,000 towards the construction of the boardwalks through Avatar Grove. Similarly, when the American outdoor gear company Patagonia opened a Victoria location, it decided to commit 1 percent of the store's sales—which the company typically donates to environmental non-profits—to the Ancient Forest Alliance. On the wall of its store hung a photo of Big Lonely Doug.

Perhaps less expectedly, the feminine hygiene company o.b. released a social media advertisement promoting its more environmentally friendly, applicator-free tampons.

"A woman uses 10,000 of these in her lifetime," the ad read, showing a graphic of an applicator. "That's 18x the height of Big Lonely Doug in British Columbia." And there it was, the unmistakable big tree, with its branch that looks like a flexed arm, silhouetted in white over o.b.'s iconic teal branding. The ad concluded with o.b.'s trademarked catchphrase: "Only what you need, nothing you don't."

The commercial wasn't met with universal praise. "How much bleach and chemicals go into your tampons? How much plastic? What are you doing for reforestation efforts? Do you use tree farms or old growth trees?" one commenter questioned under the ad. "DIVA CUP all the way!!!!! Why not save ALL the trees," another posted, referring to the reusable silicone alternative. Another commenter was simply shocked that this single tree standing in a valley near Port Renfrew had been used in such an unlikely marketing campaign: "I can't believe lonely Doug was just featured in a tampon commercial."

To some activists, there is a danger with focusing on a single tree and ignoring the forest. These charismatic arboreal protagonists can become so big on their own, they cast the issue they represent into shadow. People become tree-centric — focusing on individual trees and not the entire ecosystem. Tourists journey to see the record-breakers while driving past a clear-cut or a second-growth forest or even an old-growth forest without stopping.

In 2015, the AFA applied to the South Coast Recreation District branch of the Ministry of Forests, Lands and Natural Resource Operations to turn Big Lonely Doug into a recreational reserve. The organization needed approval if it wanted to construct a wooden viewing platform around the tree to protect its roots and base from visitors. Recreational reserve applications often come from environmental activist groups, but also from non-commercial recreation clubs hoping to build a dirt bike trail or an informal ski run, or from regional districts looking to increase tourist opportunities in their communities. They must show they will manage the site, repair boardwalks and trails, and oversee any facilities. Unlike Parks Canada, the recreation site system is not a conservation model but one that works in conjunction with various resource players.

Big Lonely Doug was approved as a recreational reserve, meaning that if a timber application, a mineral claim, or a hydroelectric proposal for the tree's immediate area is ever submitted, the recreation officer will be notified. If it is promoted to a recreational site, while the designation affords little in the way of formal protection, it would allow an organization like the Ancient Forest Alliance to legally begin constructing trails and boardwalks. The organization had received approval in 2012 for Avatar Grove to be promoted from a recreational reserve to a full recreational site, and soon began to enjoy marketing by the Ministry of Tourism.

When the application for a recreational reserve around Big Lonely Doug was circulated, representatives of the Pacheedaht First Nation approved but Teal Jones expressed concern about the bridge over the Gordon River leading to the tree. The company has moved its operations elsewhere in the valley, stating no immediate plan of returning to the spur road along the river, and so would not be maintaining the bridge. They posted bright yellow signs informing visitors that visitors assume all liability for using the road and bridge. Their concern was that if Big Lonely Doug was turned into a formal recreational site, where it would be developed with a trail and viewing platform and benefit from official provincial advertising, the bridge wouldn't be stable enough for more tourists, despite being built to carry fully loaded logging trucks. The short guardrail would need to be updated. Some saw the move by the company as a tactic to discourage people from making the pilgrimage to see the solitary tree.

The application revealed a paradox: the timber company would only update and manage the bridge if there were plans for them to return to work in the neighbouring cutblocks, including the grove of old growth next to Big Lonely Doug. The only way the tree could be granted full provincial protection in becoming a formal recreational site was if the timber company returned to clear-cut more old-growth forest at the base of Edinburgh Mountain.

CHAPTER 11

Tall Tree Capital

IN PORT RENFREW, with the successful launch of their Big Lonely Doug campaign, resulting in a furor of local interest and tourism, TJ Watt and Ken Wu began to see a movement building. They noticed two factors were resonating most strongly with the public: emotion and money. Civil disobedience can often be swept aside by government injunction or dismissed by the conservative end of the public spectrum, but when environmental issues are entrenched in business, there exists economic incentive for change. These trees could be transformative, they thought, not just for their cause but for an entire town and region, as a "first-rate potential destination" for tourists.

Port Renfrew is a place where two rivers meet—the

San Juan from the east and the Gordon from the north—and spill their melt and rain water, carried from deep inside the island, into the plunging harbour of Port San Juan. In the fall, salmon return to the harbour's head and hurl themselves into the air on their soldier-like march upriver to spawn and die. Black bears feed along the shores. Bald eagles survey the coastline from atop droopy cedars. Elk and deer graze in the grassy marshes and estuaries. Cougars and wolves lurk in the forests.

But the soggy and wind-beaten town would not exist if not for its bounty of big trees. The region's first colonial logging activity was carried out in the 1880s by Alfred Deakin, who cut trees in the Gordon River Valley and shipped timber from the port. The region's logging industry was a modest venture until 1914, when the British Columbia Lumber Company and a crew of 125 opened a camp not far from present-day Avatar Grove. In 1929, a shingle mill began operation in town, and ever since, Port Renfrew has revolved around timber—every one of its residents in some way connected to bringing trees down.

For a century, all focus was on harvesting the great trees and shipping timber from its port. Planks, beams, posts, and raw logs were loaded onto ships bound for mills and markets in urban hubs, including Victoria, Vancouver, and Seattle. In the 1930s, a rail line was built that extended twenty-two kilometres to access the heart of the region's finest timber stands. One rail trestle over Bear Creek was used so frequently that uneasy train crews would disembark, send one conductor across the bridge, and let the train pass unmanned—fearful that the bridge might give way and the load would topple into the river. Numerous logging camps were erected around Port Renfrew: along Bear Creek, Harris Creek, and the Gordon River. For decades, the town remained a backwater, a bustling but isolated community.

But through most of its history, the town existed in a liminal space. When its first post office was established in 1895, mail addressed to Port San Juan—the original name of the settlement—was erroneously being delivered to the San Juan Islands, an archipelago belonging to the United States, southeast of Vancouver Island. At the urging of the perturbed postmaster, the settlement was renamed, after Baron Renfrew, one of the titles held by the Prince of Wales.

It wasn't until 1958 that a road was extended north from Jordan River, pushing through the coastal forest to finally connect Port Renfrew with Victoria. Up until then, residents relied on weekly ships for supplies. Still, for decades the road remained a treacherous track—weaving along the jagged coast, up and down gulley, and across rickety bridges over creeks and rivers until finally the port came into view. Drivers would pass a concrete guardrail on which someone had painted: "Hang on to your beer!"

While the town remained a timber hub, most outsiders came to Port Renfrew to hike along one of the most famous trails in the world. Across the bay is the southern terminus of the West Coast Trail, a seventy-five-kilometre hike that draws thousands of visitors every year. The path was originally a trade and travel route used by coastal First Nations, and was adopted by early colonists as a telegraph trail to assist survivors of shipwrecks. This stretch of coastline was known as the Graveyard of the Pacific because of the frequency of ships hitting rocky reefs in the mist. In 1973, the hiking trail was incorporated into Pacific Rim National Park. Port Renfrew either bids good luck to trekkers setting forth, smelling fresh and with an eager spring in their step, or welcomes them out of the trail at the conclusion of their week-long hike—sore, wet, muddy, hunched, and hungry. Here, in one of the wettest places in Canada, rain falls two out of every three days a year.

The region was also known for attracting people looking to live freely off the land. Since the 1960s, Sombrio Beach, just south of Port Renfrew and one of the coastline's premier surfing destinations, had been a draw for squatters, back-to-the-landers, and free-spiriters looking for a co-operative but disengaged-from-the-world way of living. What started as a few ramshackle huts grew into a small community along one of the most postcard-perfect crescents of sand anywhere on the island—people living off Crown or unused private lands for free. One couple raised eleven children along Sombrio. But in 1996, with the establishment of the Juan de Fuca Provincial Park and a sister route to the West Coast Trail south of Port Renfrew, the Juan de Fuca Trail, the squatters were evicted. Those tied to the area moved to Port Renfrew. But throughout the coastal community, the lure of escaping still hangs in the air: you can disappear among the misty forests or at least have your unwanted past carried away by the waves and wind.

By the middle of the 1980s, the B.C. timber industry was worth more than $20 billion per year, but increasingly this money was being centralized into a handful of companies. Throughout the 1980s and '90s, smaller companies merged to form conglomerates that controlled increasingly large tree farm licences across the island. Like many once-bustling timber towns, some with mills that supported near-entire communities, Port Renfrew saw its jobs dry up and its population shrink to just a few hundred people.

An hour down coast, the seaside community of Jordan River met a similar fate. It had been a bustling logging community since it was established in the 1880s, around seventy kilometres up the coast from the

Hudson's Bay trading post turned provincial capital of Victoria. With upwards of a thousand residents, who flourished up until the 1970s, Jordan River kept as its mainstay the shipping of logs south to the mills that had opened in Victoria and Vancouver. But Jordan River also began to dwindle in the 1980s, to approximately one-tenth its size—eventually becoming known more for surfing than logging. The area has since been deemed the most seismic-prone region in British Columbia, with the so-called Big One expected along the West Coast. Out of fear that the hydroelectric project upriver, built by the Vancouver Island Power Company in 1911, would breach if a magnitude 9.0 earthquake struck the region, BC Hydro bought out nearly all of the remaining residents, effectively turning the community into a ghost town.

While some timber jobs in Port Renfrew held in certain sectors, such as contract fallers, the town started seeing an upturn in a different form of commercial interest beginning around 2010. A new wave of business erupted in town—one centred around the value not of trees lying on the ground but the value of the ones left standing.

"The trees give name to Port Renfrew," said Dan Hagar, who was elected president of the town's chamber of commerce in 2013. "People are coming not just for the trees, but also the reason they know about

Renfrew is because of the trees." Over his time as chamber president, he noticed thousands of tourists making the drive north along Highway 14, not just to hike the famous West Coast Trail or fish the shoals off coast, but to head inland to stand under some of the largest trees in the world.

Since the boom began, Port Renfrew has been heralded as "the next Tofino," a nod to the thriving surfing destination up coast that shot to global recognition following the protests in Clayoquot Sound. For Ken Wu, Tofino became a model for turning a former timber town into a tourist destination in the wake of an environmental movement, where "with every arrest, the community's GDP went up."

In marketing Port Renfrew, however, the Ancient Forest Alliance found that their early supporters were people already inclined to be voices for old-growth forest protection. So, rather than repeating the tired adage of trees versus jobs, the AFA took a different approach to court the skeptical. The organization held talks and slide shows at restaurants and cafés in town, where timber workers and environmentalists, residents old and new, met face to face. So often these duelling groups only see each other through the windshield of a logging truck as it speeds past hauling a load of timber, while activists are out searching for big trees or embarking on trail-building expeditions. Instead, the AFA positioned themselves not as the truck-blocking tree-huggers of old, but as an organization that was concerned with the future of the trees as well as the people and communities that depended on them.

But to many in Port Renfrew, including Dan Hagar, "the next Tofino" moniker is despised. For him, a more appropriate comparison for the rapid rise in development and attention in Port Renfrew lies on the mainland, not Tofino but Whistler. Tofino is a five-hour drive from Victoria, or a three-hour drive from the nearest mainland-connected ferry. Whistler—one of the most renowned ski and snowboard destinations in the world—is easily accessible to Vancouver urbanites, just an hour-and-a-half drive north of the city. For those looking for outdoor recreation—skiing and snowboarding in the winter; hiking and climbing in the summer—Whistler is far enough away for an escape, but close enough to reach after work on a Friday evening. Hagar started seeing Port Renfrew, just a two-hour drive north along the coastal highway from Victoria, in roughly the same place as where Whistler was in the 1980s: a beautifully set location that is both close to a major urban centre and well connected by multiple access roads, and somewhere that offers a bounty of outdoor activities and growing amenities. In 2010, Port Renfrew launched the Tall Tree Music Festival, a weekend-long, early summer gathering of local and international bands and musicians, who perform on a stage erected in a clear-cut now just down the road from Avatar Grove and Big Lonely Doug.

Born on the Saskatchewan prairies, Hagar moved to the West Coast and purchased a single cottage in a development that was being built out of an old campground in the summer of 2010. By 2012, he had purchased four and started a business, Handsome Dan's, which manages rental units and cottages. Many of the sea-view cottage owners live out of town—a niche in property management that Hagar stumbled upon by chance. He now runs the logistics—booking, cleaning, servicing—of more than forty rental properties, and has seen the town's exponential growth first-hand. His revenue in 2016 was ten times what it was in 2012. Thanks in part to the popularity of the big trees and the activist campaigns creating interest, local hotels and bed and breakfasts have seen a surge in demand and revenue.

"Think about how much money we would have had to spend in order to get the advertising we got as a result of Avatar Grove, Big Lonely Doug, the controversy around logging in the Walbran," Hagar said. "It was probably in the hundreds of millions of dollars in the amount of advertising that we got for Port Renfrew organically."

Two days after the Ancient Forest Alliance issued the press release announcing Big Lonely Doug, Hagar registered biglonelydoug.com and mapped the domain so that any clicks redirected to the webpage of his cottage rental management business.

IN DECEMBER 2015, the Port Renfrew Chamber of Commerce called for a moratorium on logging old growth in the region, citing the business and tourism potential of keeping the big trees standing. The statement, clear and direct, came as a paradox to some residents: the chamber is meant to support businesses, the largest of which—in thousands of small towns up and down Vancouver Island and across British Columbia—has always been timber. But the statement signalled the beginning of a shift across the province. The town of Port Renfrew stood tall, and British Columbia followed. Six months later, the B.C. Chamber of Commerce, representing 36,000 businesses across the province, passed a resolution calling on the provincial government to increase old-growth protection, stating, "The local economies stand to receive a greater net economic benefit over the foreseeable future by keeping their nearby old-growth forests standing." They cited Big Lonely Doug as an example.

The chamber also noted an economic analysis conducted by a kayaking company located in the Discovery Islands, between Vancouver Island and the mainland.

When, in 2012, a logging company expressed interest in cutting sixty hectares of old-growth forest, which would have negatively impacted the tourism industry, the kayaking company crunched the numbers on this particular plot of trees. If logged, the sixty hectares would initially produce a timber value of $3,600,000—or $60,000 per year over the sixty-year regeneration cycle until the forest could be harvested again. The kayaking company, however, was earning $416,000 per year off of operations around the un-logged islands, which would amount to $24,960,000 over the same sixty-year period. To harvest the sixty hectares, the logging company would provide three hundred full-time days of employment, while the kayaking company would provide 20,160 days of employment if the trees were left standing. In addition, the numbers cited were for just one tourism company—and forty were in operation in the region.

The B.C. Chamber of Commerce recommended to the provincial government to "support the increased protection of old-growth forests in areas of the province where they have or can likely have a greater net economic value for communities if they are left standing for the next generation and beyond" and "protect endangered old-growth forests by enacting new regulations such as an Old-Growth Management Area, Wildlife Habitat Area, or Land Use Order, with the intent to eventually legislate permanent protection for areas through provincial park or conservancies." To activists it was seen as an enormous win to gain the support of a significant provincial business body.

Still, before the year was out, timber workers and companies protested, forcing the B.C. Chamber of Commerce to issue a follow-up release titled, "B.C. Chamber Does Not Support Ban on Old-Growth Logging." To "clarify its policy position on conservation of old-growth forests," it stated that while the chamber maintained support for conservation in communities where the tourism potential is high, it also supported the province's "vibrant forestry industry," which creates jobs, powers the economy, and is "world-renowned for its sustainable forest management practices." The win, such as it was, came and went swiftly.

Dan Hagar and the Port Renfrew Chamber of Commerce decided on another approach, by redesigning the town's tourist brochure to highlight the one feature that was rapidly becoming the region's principal draw. They came up with a moniker for the town: Canada's Tall Tree Capital. The brochure included driving directions and a map, developed by the AFA, to Avatar Grove and the area's largest trees, including Big Lonely Doug. On the back cover was a picture, taken by TJ Watt, of the solitary Douglas fir.

All the big trees near Port Renfrew—and all the

other great firs, cedars, and spruces across Vancouver Island, in the forests of Carmanah and Walbran and Avatar Grove — grow within intact forests. Their trunks appear smaller when surrounded by other trees, and their heights shorter with undergrowth growing around them. Their tops are often obscured by a canopy. None of these trees, as tall or as wide or as gnarly as they are, create the stark contrast that sets Big Lonely Doug apart: one of Canada's largest trees standing alone in a clear-cut.

Sold at the small gift shop in Port Renfrew, novelty T-shirts read, "Port Renfrew: a drinking town with a fishing problem." While some of the West Coast's best fishing can be found along the rocky shores, a more fitting shirt for the future of Port Renfrew might be: "A logging town with a big-tree problem."

Port Renfrew — and the valleys that extend inland, including San Juan, Gordon, and Walbran — were becoming ground zero for the new battle over Vancouver Island's remaining old-growth forests. The region had the most to gain, and the most to lose.

WHILE MANY FAMILIES AND businesses have profited from the rebranding of Port Renfrew as the Tall Tree Capital, the benefits have only helped the Pacheedaht First Nation in a small measure. Years before Dennis

Cronin flagged cutblock 7190, Bear Charlie walked that forest along the Gordon River looking for CMTs—a bark strip tree or maybe even the remnants of a dugout canoe. Originally from Ahousaht First Nation in Clayoquot Sound, he moved to the Port Renfrew area to work on the Pacheedaht's culturally modified tree crew, and was hired by Teal Jones as part of the company's CMT requirement before clear-cutting began in cutblock 7190. He undoubtedly walked under the branches of the second-largest Douglas fir in the country, but the great tree didn't register as anything special to him or his crew partner.

"When we go in, we go more for the cedar content," he said. He found several CMTs within the cutblock.

The Pacheedaht have been managing their forest resources since long before the arrival of Europeans, but amid pressure from timber companies and activists they have remained primarily concerned with the prosperity of their people. In the spring of 2017, the First Nation opened a sawmill near Port Renfrew, minutes down the road from Avatar Grove. Jeff Jones, chief of the Pacheedaht First Nation, asked Ken Wu and the Ancient Forest Alliance if they wanted to go on a tour. Wu expected that they might head out to walk through an old-growth forest. Instead, Jones wanted to show him their mill.

"It was the most spectacular ancient cedars that

they're milling," Wu said. "It was essentially Avatar Grove laying down on its side in their yard."

The mill buys logs from local tree farm licence holders, including Teal Jones, as well as private landholders. Rather than two-by-fours, pulpboard, shakes, or other low-value lumber products, the Pacheedaht mill is turning the old-growth cedar logs into larger dimensional timbers that are sold to a supplier on Vancouver Island. They are making the best use they can out of their wood.

The tour was eye-opening for Wu, not only to see such large trees lying waiting for the saw, but because it showed that First Nations can simultaneously be advocates and allies for old-growth forest protection while also profiting from its timber. Ken Wu sees a simple way forward where both values can be protected: taking a portion of the "stumpage fees" that timber companies pay to the provincial government, and redirecting the money to non-timber revenue generation for First Nations. Wu has been proposing the option for years. But the mill offered the Pacheedaht something tangible and immediate that the activists didn't: jobs. Seasonal employment in tourism may help a few, but their mill provided year-round jobs for 10 percent of the entire nation.

Jones has tried to remain "neutral" when the Pacheedaht have been placed between environmental activists and timber companies. "We as a nation are trying to benefit from the resource itself by providing stable jobs, even if that has to do with harvesting old growth," he has said. The area that became Avatar Grove was well known to the Pacheedaht for centuries before Watt noticed the candelabra tops in the winter of 2009; their seasonal fishing camp had been located at the site long before either activists or loggers arrived. While the nation supports the desire to create more recreation sites, there is also a degree of caution.

Bear Charlie would chuckle at some of the activists' tactics. In one location in the Walbran Valley, activists had camped out in the trees in a forest that the logging company had already set aside for the Pacheedaht to manage. "They were protesting something that was already saved," he said. The logging trucks just drove by, knowing that their company had no intention of entering that particular stand. But Charlie also has had serious concerns: "If you're not going to monitor your own Avatar Grove, you're destroying it just as much as a logging company—just in different ways." He has seen tourists walking off trail, relieving themselves in the forest, and camping at the site. "You're not doing the same damage that a logging company does, but at the same time the company is coming back later to replant when they cut." He heard talk about the AFA hiring Pacheedaht guides for Avatar Grove—in a similar way that Parks Canada has hired Indigenous people to be guardians of the West Coast Trail—but it never materialized.

To Jeff Jones, there's a more fundamental issue for his nation than squabbling over individual trees or specific groves. "Our vision here is to get as much control of our territory as possible, by either management or ownership," he said. "That's our ultimate goal." Activists and loggers have been fighting over the forests for a few decades, but the Indigenous peoples of Vancouver Island have watched these forests ebb and flow for millennia. Many see the trees on a much longer time-continuum. In 2005, the Pacheedaht launched a four-hundred-year cedar conservation plan, where a percentage of tree farm licence holdings of existing old growth, or replanted forests that are at least ninety years old, is set aside by timber companies for the Pacheedaht. One of the biggest contributors of old growth and second growth to this conservation plan has been Teal Jones, the holder of TFL 46.

The companies started by setting aside individual trees, but the nation wanted forests—small areas with good cedar of various ages that would be ideal for the nation's future use. To some on the outside, opening a mill was self-interested, without regard for supporting old-growth protection; but for more than a century the nation has seen timber companies harvest trees off their traditional lands with little or no say. Jones is looking ahead—at the urgent needs of his people, as well as hundreds of years in the future and the generations to come. The immediate goal is to keep the mill operating, even if stalwart environmentalists might not entirely agree with the kinds of trees that are sawn.

Jones has seen the benefits that increased big-tree tourism can bring to the Pacheedaht-run campground that spans a crescent beach at the head of Port San Juan, and to the restaurants and services in town, but he has been cautious about blindly supporting Victoria-based activists who market a portion of forest, encourage people to visit, promote their cause, and then leave the tourists unmanaged. There have never been official guides at Avatar Grove, no signs with rules or historical information, and no washrooms. The nation has not opposed the creation of recreational sites, but questions who benefits.

"There is a fine line between conservation and economics," said Pacheedaht representative Kristine Pearson. "The activists do really well as a non-profit, and individually they make careers out of the issue."

For Jones and others in the nation, the phrase "old-growth forest" is a construction that holds less weight than it does for activists or timber companies or governments. It is a recent phrase as well, when looking through at a forest through a lens of at least four hundred years. Even a replanted cutblock of knee-high seedlings will eventually return to resemble those untouched by commercial logging, with enough of the one element that has always defined these forests: time.

CHAPTER 12

A New Ecosystem

AMONG THE BLACK BEARS and towering trees, the ferns and fungi, a new ecosystem has emerged from the forests of Vancouver Island. There are forces strong and weak, cataclysmic movements and hidden repercussions. There are threads that form connections that could be severed in an instant, or gradually eroded over the near-imperceptible passing of time.

This ecosystem includes the rights of Indigenous peoples to monitor and manage their lands and resources. It includes timber workers concerned with getting their jobs done, providing for their families, and keeping their communities afloat. It includes activists and environmentalists who fight to protect rapidly dwindling habitats and species, and who seek a compromise with an industry that has enjoyed an unchecked reign for nearly all of its existence. This new ecosystem also includes businesses looking to the forests for new sources of revenue; tourism companies using the icon of the tree to promote resilience, determination, and strength; and towns rebranding, transforming themselves from places that value their trees cut and horizontal to places that value forests left intact and standing. At the heart of this ecosystem stands Big Lonely Doug.

It has been rare that individuals in nature transcend their ecosystem. For our oceans there was Moby Doll, an orca intended to be killed and used as the model for an exhibit at the Vancouver Aquarium, but which instead was harpooned off the Gulf Islands and dragged across the Strait of Georgia to the city. Over less than two months in 1964, tens of thousands of visitors came to see the "blackfish"—a beast from the depths—struggle to survive in a makeshift dockyard enclosure. But in its brief time as one of the first orcas in captivity, the whale came to symbolize our quest to capture and train these animals for show and profit, as well as to represent the spark to further understand and protect them.

For our north there was Knut, the polar bear that never walked free. In 2006, a cub was born in the Berlin Zoological Garden that was rejected by its mother. The animal quickly became a media sensation, with approximately four hundred reporters covering the cub's public unveiling. But when an animal rights activist suggested that Knut should have been put down rather than raised by humans, protests erupted. At age four, the first polar bear to survive past infancy at the facility died, with the zoo stating that Knut's untimely passing was due to "significant changes to the brain, which could be seen as the reason for the sudden death," and PETA claiming the animal had gone "crazy." Over his short life, Knut not only became beloved but was registered as a trademark by the Berlin zoo, generated more than $7 million in revenue, and was photographed by Annie Leibovitz for *Vanity Fair*'s Green Issue.

For our forests there is Big Lonely Doug, a survivor standing resolute. No matter the storm, whether nature's wrath or human greed, that courses through these valleys, life can endure if given a chance.

MANY PEOPLE SPECULATED AS to why a logger, whose job it was to extract as much monetary value from the forests as possible, would save such an enormous tree. The most common assumption is that Big Lonely Doug was left as a wildlife tree, a specimen of great age set aside by timber companies to help reseed a cutblock. The Ancient Forest Alliance's initial press release stated that Teal Jones likely left the tree in order to satisfy requirements for "variable retention" timber harvesting, a practice where individual trees or clumps of trees are left standing in a cutblock in order to maintain diversity of species and age. If a few of the older trees are kept, it is thought, the forest will at least carry on some of its ecological heritage. The practice was introduced in 1995 by the Clayoquot Scientific Panel in the wake of the War in the Woods protests. According to the B.C. Ministry of Forests, "The broader focus of retaining structure within the stand results in the maintenance of a much wider variety of forest values, including wildlife habitat and aesthetics. In short, the retention system shifts the management focus from what can be removed to what can be retained."

It is a timber harvesting practice that has never sat well with activists. The AFA wondered if Teal Jones had left Big Lonely Doug in an attempt to absolve themselves of the "clear-cutting" label. Variable retention harvesting, however, has set restrictions, chief among them being that at least half of a cutblock's trees must be retained, each within a tree height of each other. If the trees are approximately thirty metres tall, for example, that much space must be left between. Leaving one or a few scattered individual trees in a cutblock would not qualify. While the terms are not synonymous, "variable retention" is what most people imagine when they hear the words "selective logging," which is where loggers remove only some of the trees in a forest and leave a substantial portion remaining to reseed, maintain age diversity, and retain at least some of the structural integrity of the forest.

In 1995, the provincial government also released the *Biodiversity Guidebook*, a lengthy set of recommendations for forest engineers, planners, and managers to meet ecological goals outlined in the Forest Practices Code of British Columbia Act. The guidebook was meant to be exactly that, a guide with practices "designed to reduce the impacts of forest management on biodiversity, within targeted social and economic constraints." It defines a "wildlife tree" as

> any standing live or dead tree with special characteristics that provide valuable habitat for conservation or enhancement of wildlife. These trees have characteristics such as large size (diameter and height) for site, condition, age, and decay stage; evidence of use; valuable species types; and relative scarcity. They serve as critical habitat (for denning, shelter, roosting, and foraging) for a wide variety of organisms such as vertebrates, insects, mosses, and lichens.

The spectrum of nine categories described in the *Biodiversity Guidebook* runs from a dead, branchless tree—commonly called a "standing snag"—that offers habitats for insects and amphibians, to a healthy tree with no decay or rot that is ideal for reseeding a cutblock. Above all, the guidebook marks the oldest and largest trees as the best candidates for retention and recommends that they are left at the edges of a cutblock, incorporated into a riparian buffer. Timber companies prefer to leave trees along the perimeters as well. Loggers have to work around a wildlife tree standing in the middle of a cutblock, and it can often be damaged during the process. While companies may not suppress the inclination to save certain trees, they are far from encouraging of the practice. Forest workers are under no requirement to set aside a particular number or percentage of individual or clusters of trees within a cutblock. It is left to the discretion of the logger.

When Dennis Cronin wrapped a green ribbon around the big fir in cutblock 7190, it was not without precedent. Like many timber workers, Cronin was not immune to pressure once the confrontations between environmental activists and loggers that had occurred predominantly on Haida Gwaii, then the Queen Charlotte Islands, in the late 1980s, began expanding to Vancouver Island—especially when conflict erupted near his hometown of Lake Cowichan.

"Everybody was trying to get dirt on you all the time," he said. "They had cameras on you."

The job became scrutinized by the media and by the public. Cronin looked back at Carmanah and the War in the Woods as a pivotal moment that sparked much-needed change. The industry needed a shakeup, he said. In the wake of these movements, Cronin and his partner Walter Van Hell began saving more trees, usually ones on the edges of a cutblock that held little value to their company. On one job in the Cowichan Valley, the pair left a patch of trees surrounding a Douglas fir nearly as large as Big Lonely Doug. On another, he worked in a small cutblock that held more than fifteen bear dens, including some several metres off the ground in slits in the side of large hollow cedars. It was impossible not to be affected by the realization that after leaving a cutblock, the inevitability of logging would set in.

Just outside Port Renfrew, Van Hell helped promote the formal protection of an approximately eighty-metre-tall Sitka spruce growing within a thin sliver of forest sandwiched between Harris Creek and the road that connects the town to Lake Cowichan. In his office and among friends, the tree was known as the Van Hell Spruce, but it was eventually named the Harris Creek Spruce.

Dennis Cronin and Walter Van Hell weren't alone in their desire to protect a few exceptional trees. Just outside Victoria, along the Koksilah River grew a stand of Douglas firs that held some towering and ancient specimens. Without the damp and fruitful conditions of the west coast of the island, the trees on the south-eastern rim of Vancouver Island grow more slowly. One Douglas fir near the river, while only forty-five metres tall, was deemed by MacMillan Bloedel as worthy of a bronze plaque. Affixed on October 4, 1957, it noted the Douglas fir "is believed to be the oldest living tree of its kind in Canada." The tree blew down in the winter of 1985, allowing it to be dated at 1,340 years old. The plaque also mentioned that "the area is now set aside to remain in its natural state." Later reports stated the plaque could "no longer be found."

By the late 1980s, patches of untouched coastal Douglas fir forest similar to Koksilah Grove were rapidly dwindling across Vancouver Island. But the value remained. In the spring of 1989, the timber company that had assumed timber rights in the Shawnigan Lake region sent two of its fallers into what had become known as Koksilah Grove. But the grove growing alongside the Koksilah River was supposed to have already been protected. Apart from MacMillan Bloedel's bronze plaque, a forest engineer named Don McMullan had recommended two years prior that a small patch of forest around the largest trees be set aside, but the recommendation was supposedly misplaced. And so the timber company, Fletcher Challenge, sent in its fallers. Don Hughes and Louie Van Beers were immediately struck not only by the grandeur of the forest but by the rarity of such old Douglas firs. Defiantly, the two men put down their saws and refused to cut the stand.

"You don't find old-growth timber like this anymore," Van Beers told the *Times Colonist*. "There are old firs seven to eight feet through, and some cedar. It is very accessible to the public and alongside the river. And we both felt they could put aside a little piece of that." With mounting public pressure, Fletcher Challenge agreed not to cut four hectares of trees along the river and mark it as a land reserve. It was a company designation that was little more than a promise not to harvest that particular area.

For two decades, timber companies paid little attention to the patch of great firs growing along the Koksilah River. Locals continued to enjoy recreating along the river and under the trees, until 2007 when a hiker, to his surprise, noticed a logging road that appeared to have been recently laid out, and trees flagged with ribbon and sprayed with light blue paint—clear signs of imminent logging activity. Once again, another company was pushing forward plans to log Koksilah. Amid renewed public and media pressure, the company relented—agreeing to set aside the patch of forest—and the provincial Ministry of Forests placed the Koksilah Grove on its list for park acquisition.

Modern environmental activists often point to the

story of the Koksilah Grove as a cautionary tale of why timber companies cannot be trusted with policing or protecting the forests. Their word, or even a company designation such as "wildlife zone" or "wildlife tree," holds no formal protection and offers no assurance to those fighting for their conservation. A plaque can disappear in a windstorm, paperwork can be misplaced in the turmoil of acquisition and merger, and the story of the dissenting act of two timber workers can fade from memory.

Dennis Cronin didn't flag the big Douglas fir in cutblock 7190 to satisfy a code or management policy for the company he worked for. It wasn't a wildlife tree in his eyes. In the end, it may help repopulate the clear-cut, dropping its feather-tail seeds from its branches, but to him the tree didn't hold any kind of future utility that could be exploited. It didn't tick a box on a form.

"It's like a legacy, ya know?" Cronin said, four years after he saved the tree. "You're saving something special. Even though I'm a logger and I've taken out millions of trees, you won't see anything like these trees again."

In a March 18, 1923, article in the *New York Times*, a reporter asked British climber George Mallory, after two unsuccessful expeditions to attempt to climb Mount Everest, why he wanted to try again the following year—why the alpinist felt compelled to summit the tallest mountain in the world. "Because it's there,"

Mallory is quoted as saying. The now-legendary retort has been called "the most famous three words in mountaineering," and reduced the world's greatest sporting feat to its fundamental motivations. The climber didn't need a grand reason. He didn't need to make a point or push a cause. He didn't need to puff his chest or inflate his accomplishments. He just had a job to do: put on his spiked boots and step into the mountains.

A foreman on the crew that was hauling the logs from cutblock 7190 asked Dennis Cronin why he saved that particular tree. Cronin offered a response with a similar rationale.

"Because I liked it," he said.

THROUGHOUT HIS CAREER, Dennis Cronin stumbled upon other unusual finds while working in the forests of Vancouver Island. He noticed countless examples of Indigenous people using the trees as a resource: holes that had been drilled into cedars to test their density; or stacks of cedar shakes, split and ready to use to construct houses. On one occasion, he found an unfinished ocean canoe partially dug out of a felled cedar located two and a half kilometres from the coast. The Indigenous carver had sought out the most ideal piece of timber, even if it would produce a canoe that would eventually have to be hauled through thick forest for days to be launched at the shoreline. But the canoe had been abandoned—likely from a defect that had appeared in the wood—more than a century ago, Cronin estimated, judging by the one-hundred-year-old tree that was growing out of the log.

"They were just starting to carve it out, but left it," Cronin said. "It was *exactly* ten metres."

He uncovered pre–European-contact stone tools and hundreds of culturally modified trees. On October 23, 2013, while surveying a patch of forest on a mountainside overlooking Port Renfrew, he stumbled upon a remarkable archaeological find: the wreckage of an airplane. Cronin and his partners had just laid out a cutblock near the top of a mountain, which held less timber than they were expecting, when they began cruising down the slope in search of a high-value stand that could be incorporated. As Cronin scrambled down through the salal bushes, he spotted bright yellow among the green and brown. He picked up a piece of twisted aluminium and called to his co-workers, including his partner Walter Van Hell.

"There's an airplane here!" Cronin yelled out.

One piece of metal led to another, and another even larger still, until the timber workers were surrounded by fragments of a fuselage, wings, and two distinct propeller engines. The wreck looked old, overgrown as if it had been there for decades.

By happenstance Cronin had solved a decades-old mystery: the disappearance of Avro Anson L7056, a Second World War–era British training aircraft that had vanished. Just after 9 a.m. on October 30, 1942, the plane had taken off from RCAF Station Patricia Bay, now the site of Victoria International Airport, on a three-hour navigational training flight. It never returned. A number of other planes had been lost at sea during similar exercises; the same was assumed to have happened to L7056, but Cronin's discovery proved otherwise. The pilot had likely become disoriented in the thick fog that often forms a bank along the coastline and crashed into the forested mountains just inland. The aircraft would have entered the forest like a lightning bolt, carving a line through the trees before disintegrating. Four airmen, two of them just twenty-one years old, died.

Within a sprawling debris field spread throughout the forest, the three timber workers found a leather boot, a first-aid kit, and what looked like a bomb protruding from the earth. The men left the wreck and called the RCMP. Seventy-one years to the day after the plane crashed, they led members of the Canadian Forces to the site, which had been kept from the public to ensure artefact hunters wouldn't prowl the wreckage looking for trinkets, and closed the chapter on an enduring mystery.

But of all Cronin's findings, it was the big Douglas fir

in cutblock 7190 that stood out. During that sunny winter day in 2011, he unintentionally created a monument that is drawing pilgrims away from the famed coastlines and over to the frontlines of old-growth logging in the heart of Vancouver Island.

"Back in the day, that tree would've been cut down," Cronin said. "I'm glad it grabbed everybody's attention. Nobody would have ever seen it if we hadn't logged that piece."

It is a statement—that logging was responsible for revealing the second-largest Douglas fir in the country—that is hard to hear for activists like TJ Watt, who continue to spend weekend after weekend in the hope of finding and saving not just the big trees but the forests around them.

And yet if Big Lonely Doug was a twenty-metre-tall fir standing alone in a cutblock, it would not have attracted as much attention; if it was growing at the edge of a clearcut, it would not have offered such a stark image; if it was found deep in the hills of Vancouver Island, far from a town like Port Renfrew, it would never have brought so many visitors to stand at its broad base; and if the tree was found in an already-protected forest, never in danger of being cut down, it would never have been given its name nor made headlines. The tree that is known as Big Lonely Doug is a product of many factors that began when a logger stood beside its trunk and looked up.

BIG LONELY DOUG IS one of the last remaining great specimens of an endangered species. If it had the face and white fur of the spirit bear, it would have governments partnering with environmental groups to protect its habitat. If it swam in pods and leapt from the ocean like an orca, it would have documentaries made about its plight that sparked public outcry and protesters outside aquariums. But Big Lonely Doug is endangered nonetheless. It is one of the last of its kind—the great trees of Vancouver Island; an example of natural grandeur and history that will soon only be found in a few protected zones and seen by only the most intrepid among us. For now, Big Lonely Doug stands tall. The tree's thick roots, as wide as a person, draw groundwater from deep underground and up seventy metres to nourish its crown of dark green needles and the mosses, lichens, and ferns that cling to its high branches.

In the years since cutblock 7190 was logged, life has slowly returned to the barren twelve hectares alongside the Gordon River. Around the base of the great tree, huckleberry and salmonberry bushes bristle through sun-bleached fragments and dead branches of the great cedars, hemlocks, and firs that once stood shoulder to shoulder in this valley. Trees are growing there, too. The replanted seedlings are inching upwards, filling the blank space and returning green to the cutblock with every year that passes. Because life is opportunistic. The network of underground fungi will eventually return to connect the great fir's broad roots to those just starting out. Water and nutrients will begin to flow through the subterranean network to once again connect the trees.

There are other knee-high trees growing in cutblock 7190 that are undoubtedly the offspring of Big Lonely Doug. When a seed falls from a tree growing in an intact forest, it tumbles directly down through the canopy, protected from winds that otherwise can carry it afar. But for an isolated and exposed tree bearing the full brunt of the winds, its seeds may well be caught up in a torrential updraft and carried as far as a kilometre away.

There are still days every autumn when little more than a cool breeze will enter the valley and ruffle the branches and cones of the lone tree in the cutblock, dislodging seeds that tumble the sixty-six metres to the ground. Most of the tens of thousands of seeds will never sprout, finding the ground inhospitably dry or overexposed, but some will find a niche of tolerable conditions and thrive.

A forest will return to cutblock 7190. It will take decades—maybe close to a century—for the seedlings to become saplings and eventually grow into trees that will begin to fill in the blank space around Big Lonely Doug. The forest that became a clear-cut will become a crop—and the trees that will eventually surround the single towering fir will never be the same as those that once stood. The majority of the seedlings, all planted at once, will grow in unison and create an even-aged canopy that blocks the beams of sunlight that so commonly penetrate the variegation of old-growth forests. Moss and lichen and undergrowth will struggle to fully establish in the drier and darker conditions.

In several decades, these twelve hectares along the northeast bank of the Gordon River will look much like the rest of the second-growth forests found across Vancouver Island. Eventually, the replanted seedlings will mature into trees substantial enough to once again draw the attention of the timber industry. We won't let this stand grow for centuries and centuries until it begins to resemble what it once did—natural deadfall becoming nurse logs for the next generation of trees, mounds of moss and thickets of salal covering the forest floor, lichens dripping from branches—with all the depth of character that can be achieved only with time. Instead, our impatience will overrule once again. The next generation of foresters will be sent to the valley with their orange and pink flagging, to plot out the boundaries of a new cutblock and create a map depicting how the logs can be extracted. The cruisers will arrive next to assess the value of the stand, now ripe to be cut. The dollar figure will be much less than any patch of old growth that once stood on Vancouver Island, but it will be all the industry can get by that point. Machines will come next—hulking loaders and trucks will be driven across the bridge high above the Gordon River and along the road at the base of Edinburgh Mountain to their next job site. Under a new name, cutblock 7190 will be logged once again. The trees will come down more easily than the ancients that stood before, most likely with the help of a machine that can saw through the narrow trunks with ease. But before the regrown patch of forest disappears, under the canopy will walk a logger—an engineer, a timber cruiser, a faller—with a job to do. Each tree they weave around will be identical to the last, looking like stalks of giant corn growing uniformly in a field. But they will come upon one, a Douglas fir with a girth and height that dwarfs its neighbours; it will protrude from the uniform canopy like a monolith. The logger will stand under the big tree and stop—and gaze from broad base to broken top.

What kind of value will that logger see?

LIKE THE GREAT FIR HE SAVED, Dennis Cronin was the last of his kind. If the remaining old growth is eventually brought down, the generations of loggers who put axe and chainsaw to trunk will have no more great trees to cut. The West Coast fallers who stalked the forests of Vancouver Island in search of big timber will find only small trees left to cut. The shift to cutting second growth exclusively will arrive—if not by choice then by necessity—and with it a continued shift towards mechanized felling.

When that happens, Vancouver Island's old-growth legacy—save for a few scattered parks and protected areas—will be lost, and with it, any potential for communities similar to Port Renfrew to build new economies out of groves left intact and trees left vertical. And so the race continues to find Vancouver Island's last great trees. Down kilometres of logging roads, far from public view, timber workers search for pockets of dense green worth millions. Activists are on the hunt, too, for the same trees but with a different vision. They hope a few can be saved as small groves or larger forest tracts, to be preserved, enjoyed, and appreciated for centuries to come.

Over his career, Cronin saw thousands of hectares of forest up and down Vancouver Island disappear—ancient trees in great stands felled, limbed, hauled, and loaded onto trucks destined for the mill. He walked some of the grandest forests on the West Coast, and loved every second of it. After he flagged the big Douglas fir in cutblock 7190, Cronin would often return to stand beside its wide trunk and under its crooked canopy. One weekend, shortly after the clear-cut, he took his wife, Lorraine, and their friends Joe and Karen Simpson to the tree. They drove to Port Renfrew and out onto the bumpy logging roads, with Cronin describing the details of the landscape they passed and where he had worked.

"He was a master of the backroads," Joe Simpson remembered the day. "I can't tell a rose from a thorn, but he knew all the plants, all the trees, and all the flowers."

Cronin spotted a small herd of elk grazing in a marshy meadow before anyone else did.

They parked on the road and walked down into cutblock 7190, past stumps of giant cedars and firs. Cronin was proud, Karen Simpson remembered, to show them the tree that was still standing. He told his friends how there are only a few of these exceptionally large and old Douglas firs remaining on Vancouver Island. Originally from Ottawa, the Simpsons were astounded—standing back and looking up at a thousand-year-old tree more than two-thirds the height of the Peace Tower on Parliament Hill in their hometown.

"These guys that work in the lumber industry see all sorts of trees, but Dennis obviously recognized this one as a very, very special tree that should never be cut down," Joe Simpson said.

The four of them joined hands to try to encircle the tree. They came up several people short.

Sometimes Cronin and his wife took the drive from their home in Lake Cowichan to visit Big Lonely Doug.

Sometimes they brought their sons. But Cronin would always remember to pack a bag of bread for the Steller's jay. After cutblock 7190 was harvested, the jay that followed him around like a dog moved to the grove of old growth next door. The bird finally flew over the creek it would never cross—by force rather than by will—after the trees it had called home disappeared. Cronin would stand on the road alongside the droopy limbs of hemlocks and cedars, and the bird would fly out of the forest and eat from his hand.

After four decades working in the forests of Vancouver Island—first as a hooktender for a crew and then as a forest engineer—Cronin's career ended abruptly. On September 5, 2012, seven months after tying the green "LEAVE TREE" ribbon around the base of the second-largest Douglas fir in the country, he was diagnosed with colon cancer. He stopped work the following week. Like many cancer treatments, it came with ups and downs. Positive results were met with optimism; negative ones with increasing concern. He tried conventional treatments as well as non-traditional ones. As the chemicals that were fighting his disease coursed through his body, the man grew thinner. But it was a seemingly minor consequence of his disease and treatment that hit him hard—Cronin's moustache, which he hadn't shaved since he was old enough to grow one, began to fall out. He was devastated.

The town of Lake Cowichan, despite losing its mill located up the lake in the small community of Youbou in 2001, had remained a logging town through and through. The town rallied to help the Cronins. A bottle drive, where people donated their refundables, and a hot dog sale were held to raise money to help the family cover costs. Timber workers filled their trucks with scrap wood gathered from cutblocks around the Lake Cowichan and Port Renfrew area that was then split and sold as firewood to help fundraise.

Through it all, Cronin wanted desperately to return to work, to be healthy and back in the bush with his co-workers, his forests, and his peanut butter sandwiches. When treatments worked, he returned to work; it was during one of these returns, when his cancer had gone into remission, that he stumbled upon the wreck of the Avro Anson plane. But when the cancer came back, Cronin could delay his official retirement for only so long. He finally accepted that the odds were against him and that he might never return to work in the forests of Vancouver Island. He retired in the spring of 2015. Less than a year later, on April 12, 2016, Dennis Cronin died in the living room of his home in Lake Cowichan. His spike-soled logger's caulk boots and red vest lay at the ready.

The valleys of Vancouver Island can be ruthlessly windy places and the Cowichan Valley is no different.

That spring, a cool wind swirled in the valley, churning up white-capped waves on the long lake. The wind tore southwest over the hills—through ancient forest and over fresh clear-cut—towards the Pacific Ocean. It rose over Edinburgh Mountain, where Queen Charlotte goshawks caught the up-currents, twisting and turning in the air above their nests in the tallest trees. The wind rushed down the mountainside, dispersing the morning fog that hugged the trees in the Gordon River Valley before erupting into open space where a forest once stood. The wind swirled in the clear-cut and around the trunk of a single tree standing on its own. The tree's glossy green needles ruffled, its broad trunk swayed ever so gently back and forth—another force pulling at its limbs—but the tree stood. Still tied at the base of the great Douglas fir, Dennis Cronin's green ribbon fluttered in the wind.

EPILOGUE

A Giant

IT TAKES GREAT EFFORT to leave footprints in an old-growth forest in a valley on Vancouver Island, where every mark in the moss and soil from a heavy step is near-instantly absorbed. A simple stroll is always an ordeal. Vines and bramble snag at boots, damp ferns soak through pants, and every apparent way through ends up being blocked by a tree or fallen log or thicket. It is what painter Emily Carr called "perfectly ordered disorder designed with a helter-skelter magnificence."

It was a sense of the unknown — what may lie hidden around the next turn — that kept bringing TJ Watt back again and again to Port Renfrew's forests. One grey September day, Watt dipped under damp hemlock branches and into Eden Grove. This forest had always held a particular pull for him. It was where he came so close to stumbling upon the second-largest Douglas fir in the country but came too late. It was where a photograph had changed the course of his organization.

Scattered groves similar to Eden stand flagged and ready to be razed. They are tucked away down kilometres of remote logging roads across Vancouver Island, far from where the pavement ends. These forests will fall in a quiet thunder, like thousands before them.

Vancouver Island has already entered the twilight years of its old-growth logging. Most of the great trees are already gone: cut, hauled, milled, and sold. The magnificent towers of nature broken down and reassembled into great manmade towers in their stead. But the tipping point is coming. It is only a matter of time. The question of Vancouver Island's timber industry shifting from old growth to second growth is not one of *if* but *when*. The finite supply of ancient, big trees will, when exhausted, force that change. Both activists and loggers agree that the days of old-growth logging are approaching the horizon. Some say within ten years, while others more optimistically say twenty.

Like cutblock 7190, the southern half of Eden Grove was flagged and surveyed by Dennis Cronin and Walter Van Hell; their orange, pink, and red ribbons were still tied to the branches and fluttering in the light breeze. Teal Jones, the licensee for this stand of old growth, holds the power to send in fallers with their chainsaws at any moment. Watt photographed a series of pink "road location" ribbons dangling in a line through the old-growth forest like a trail of ominous breadcrumbs. It was a picture that hinted at what could come next: the thin pieces of ribbon replaced with a road cut through a previously undisturbed forest.

There is a stoicism in Watt, a self-assurance from knowing that more can be gained in the fight to protect Vancouver Island's dwindling old-growth forests by gradually and patiently taking steps forward. The best campaigns take time to conceptualize, design, and implement. Clever marketing can be as effective as bullish activism, and there is sometimes more power in a picture than in a protest.

"You go to Egypt to see the pyramids, but people are coming here to see the trees," Watt said, standing before a western red cedar nearly as burly and twisted as his Gnarly Tree. After Avatar Grove hit the news, he began receiving calls from tourists from as far as Russia, Australia, and Switzerland asking to hire him as a guide to see Port Renfrew's great trees.

The ground under his boots was spongy and sodden; the bushes of salal and huckleberry dripping with dew. He tiptoed along a fallen cedar log, slowly rotting but acting as a veritable nursery for hundreds of hemlock seedlings. Watt continued down towards the Gordon

River, farther into the forest, until a large cedar came into view through the tangle of undergrowth and trees. A metre-long slit in the tree's trunk created an opening, around which were layers of scratches and claw marks. A bear den. Watt had visited this tree often since his first forays into the forests of this valley. Nearby, a narrow creek rushing water towards the river acted as a demarcation line between the two cutblocks—between intact forest and clear-cut, between what he was fighting to protect and what had fallen, between past and future. He peered through a window in the forest made by drooping branches, and across cutblock 7190, to spot the silhouette of Big Lonely Doug against the grey sky.

Watt bent down to remove a field camera he had wired to a small cedar trunk on a previous visit. He was hoping to capture video of the black bear entering her den. He pressed play and the small LCD screen flashed on, and the one-minute video began: rain patters down through the canopy, as the mother bear lumbers into the frame next to the giant cedar with the hollow. She is quickly followed by her cub, likely born that spring, which stops suddenly in the forest after noticing the camera, a foreign object, attached eye level to a tree. The cub approaches, licks the lens, and gnaws for a second on the metal box before realizing it has fallen behind its mother. It bounds off after her. With no more motion in the frame, the video cuts to black.

The megafauna that inhabit the Pacific temperate rainforests often leave traces of their existence—scat, claw marks, dens, disturbed earth. But they remain hidden and quiet, lurking just out of sight of the humans who thrash clumsily about. But they are there. For Watt, ecstatic as he tucked the full memory card into his camera backpack, to see a mother black bear and her cub among these giant trees, their fur wet with rain, was a reminder that these forests hold value for more than just humans.

Watt descended farther into the forest, from colossal cedar to towering fir to colossal cedar, weaving through the underbrush as if he were following a well-marked trail, until he reached a pebble-bottomed creek. In a flash of blue and black, a Steller's jay landed on a mossy branch above him, looked down, and cocked its head expectedly.

AS THE ANCIENT FOREST ALLIANCE'S director, Ken Wu has always seen his job as similar to a filmmaker's. "The big trees are sort of like an actor, but you still have to have the script, the directing, the producing, and the cinematography," he says. A narrative is needed to fill in the blanks, superlatives to provide the hook, and tension to add the drama—but it all needs to be framed around a tree or grove that will evoke awe. "We can't use an encrusted lichen as the most charismatic character."

In the narrative of Big Lonely Doug, there was obvious tension, but Wu hopes his campaigns focus on the beauty rather than the destruction. "We have to include enough destruction in there that it's compelling and motivating and urgent," he says. With Avatar Grove, the layer of destruction in the narrative was a looming one—a question of what is at stake of being lost. With Big Lonely Doug, it was a glimpse of the stark reality of timber harvesting on Vancouver Island.

Arnie Bercov at the Public and Private Workers of Canada has forged a relationship with the AFA to achieve similar goals: sustainable management of British Columbia's forests as well as development of communities. Many see the friendly relationship between a labour union representing timber industry employees and an environmental activist group pushing to save the trees as an unlikely alliance—but the two organizations have found common ground at an intersection where clichéd rhetoric is replaced with no-nonsense pragmatism. The relationship has revealed that the age-old image of burly loggers facing off against dreadlocked tree-huggers is largely a construct, and the environment-versus-jobs argument a smokescreen.

While the PPWC has been supportive of the Ancient Forest Alliance's call for an increase in old-growth forest protection and a decrease of raw log exports, it is still a labour union—it represents workers and jobs above all else. For Bercov, where the provincial government has failed is not in the forests that we are not cutting but in the forests that we *are* cutting.

"If we're going to make the effort to cut a tree down," Bercov says, "then we better make sure we use it to the fullest extent."

Vancouver Island has the potential to arise as a model not just for British Columbia or Canada but North America, in which a longstanding industry based on a primary resource not only adapts to meet the changing environment but also looks to the future. It could stand as a model where healthy ecosystems and healthy timber workforces are not mutually exclusive. For Bercov, there lies potential in innovation in sustainable second-growth forestry, in investment in new mills tied to timber leases producing high-value products such as laminated beams made from second-growth trees, and in diverting stumpage fees to support Indigenous communities pursuing more diverse economic models. If properly managed, Vancouver Island's forests stand to be the epitome of a renewable resource.

"The industry is a shell of what it should be," Bercov says. "Not what it *could* be but what it *should* be." It should be creating jobs, addressing climate change, providing opportunities for the next generation, working with Indigenous communities, and seeking out alternative sources of income from our forests. It should be valuing every part of a tree—whether cut or standing.

THE VALUE THE Ancient Forest Alliance has gleaned from Big Lonely Doug, in awareness and attention, has spread their cause of protecting the region's old-growth forests well beyond Vancouver Island's coastlines. Port Renfrew's big trees have caught the eye of filmmakers and photographers around the world.

In 2016, acclaimed filmmaker and artist Kelly Richardson took a hike though Avatar Grove and found herself overwhelmed, physically and emotionally. To celebrate the fiftieth anniversary of IMAX in 2019, she partnered with Christian Kroitor, the grandson of Canadian filmmaker and IMAX co-founder Roman Kroitor, to begin filming a moving-image installation that would highlight not only the size of the region's trees but also their predicament—"why we continue to define progress through the conversion of nature."

It was an image of Big Lonely Doug that excited world-renowned environmental photographer Edward Burtynsky. Over a career dating back to the 1970s, Burtynsky, originally from St. Catharines, Ontario, has travelled around the globe producing images that are hauntingly beautiful in their depiction of destruction, corrosion, and consequence. Often shot out of a helicopter or plane window, his photographs take on an otherworldly veneer, where the subject and scene isn't immediately clear. It takes a moment to realize what exactly is in the frame. *Is that water? Is that oil? Are those trees?* And then, like a Magic Eye autostereogram, the reality comes into focus. His photography has been exhibited at the National Gallery of Canada in Ottawa, the Bibliothèque nationale in Paris, and the Guggenheim Museum in New York City.

Burtynsky starred in the 2006 documentary *Manufactured Landscapes*, set on one of his shoots in China, which took the viewer from an appliance factory to the Three Gorges Dam to highlight the impact of mass industrialization. In 2013, he co-directed *Watermark*, which visited nearly a dozen places around the world to show how water is used, consumed, and tainted by humans.

While doing research for possible subjects and locations for his next film and visual project, *Anthropocene*, Burtynsky felt that one of the more pressing issues of humans transgressing the boundaries of the planet is deforestation. He considered the forests cut for palm-oil production in Borneo and the destruction of rainforests in the Amazon—two subjects with plenty of media attention—but ultimately settled on a location closer to home: Canada's West Coast. One image and story stood out: that of a single Douglas fir left standing in the middle of a cutblock near Port Renfrew, British Columbia.

Big Lonely Doug offered an opportunity for Burtynsky to employ a new way of communicating an image and an issue. While staying true to his well-known ethos—large-scale photographs depicting the often unseen and fraught intersections where humans and environments meet—he employed new technology. Rather than trying to come away with a singular photograph that encapsulated the story, the place, and the issue, he set out to capture the tree in new ways that would highlight its scale and individuality on a level people hadn't seen before.

Over several visits to the tree, Burtynsky gathered footage for his documentary but also used a drone to capture high-resolution images of Big Lonely Doug's trunk that can be stitched together. Spanning 1.5 metres high and up to 12 metres long—the length of the tree's circumference—the image will be a life-size representation of the tree's girth that can be printed and displayed flat against the wall of a museum, business, or institution.

"It's a little more conceptual in its origins than trying to be accurately representational," Burtynsky says about the image. "It's more about trying to represent a tree in a different way."

Big Lonely Doug also presented an opportunity for

Burtynsky to represent the tree in three dimensions. Using hundreds of images he has taken of the tree, he has created an augmented reality object, where people can download an app to their smartphone or tablet, stand back, and be able to see through the camera on their device a life-size 3-D virtual image of Big Lonely Doug standing before them on the street. They will be able to walk around its massive trunk and take photos of their friends alongside the second-largest Douglas fir in the country. It could take the issue of Vancouver Island's old-growth destruction and preservation to people anywhere in the world.

"It will bring the scale of this tree into public consciousness," Burtynsky says.

Big Lonely Doug is one of several of his augmented reality installations, including a mound of automotive parts in a scrapyard in Ghana and a pile of tusks from poached elephants Burtynsky photographed in Kenya that were confiscated by officials and set alight. People will be able to walk up to and around the thousands of tusks piled twenty feet high. "It's a way to speak about extinction. And cutting down these thousand-year-old trees is the same." He hopes that his projects will inspire change, both in perspective and policy, and help spur a moratorium on old-growth logging in British Columbia. "Big Lonely Doug is a hopeful symbol. It represents that these amazing ecosystems are still among us—and that they are truly our responsibility to preserve."

If Big Lonely Doug had never been found, never flagged, and never protected, it would have lived out its natural life, no doubt as one of the last exceptionally large Douglas firs on Vancouver Island. It would never have been climbed and measured, never been added to the B.C. BigTree Registry alongside its elite brethren. It would never have been turned into a symbol, marketed, and promoted. Big Lonely Doug was erected like a tower. It was a calculated creation to highlight the plight of an entire species—the Douglas fir—of an entire landscape—the hills and valleys of Vancouver Island—and of an entire ecosystem—the Pacific temperate rainforests of Canada's West Coast.

And it has worked. Few single trees in Canada have ever enjoyed such a reputation.

Still, in a heartbeat TJ Watt would trade the single tree as it stands now for the forest that was razed around it. He still shakes his head when he thinks about how close he came, while hiking through Eden Grove mere months before Dennis Cronin, to saving both: "I went left instead of right."

For Ken Wu, so much of the forest industry and the dominant paradigm have been focused on the tree rather than the ecosystem, which has allowed the timber companies to claim that old growth can be easily replaced by plantations, and that leaving Big Lonely Doug is a fundamentally good deed. But Wu still sees value in these individual trees.

For years, Wu has been petitioning British Columbia's Liberal government to create a Big Tree Protection Order, a piece of legislation that would shield the province's biggest trees for good. Specimens of a certain diameter would be untouchable to timber companies, in recognition of their superior ecological and cultural value — above and beyond what they are worth as boards and posts. Additionally, each tree that met the size and age requirements would be left with a surrounding buffer of forest. In many areas that hold a high density of large trees, these buffer zones would overlap to effectively place the entire grove off limits to logging. In 2009, British Columbia Minister of Forests and Range Pat Bell tempered the appeal. "We're confident these trees won't be harvested," he told the *Vancouver Sun* about the record-holders listed in the BigTree Registry. "They're tagged, they're named, we know exactly where they are and we're keeping track of them... No district manager would dare approve a cutting plan or permit that would allow for the harvesting of any of these trees." But Wu wasn't concerned with those already recognized and named by the public; he was worried about the trees nobody knew about — ones that could be felled before anyone noticed.

Two years later, with public pressure mounting following the rise in popularity of Avatar Grove, Bell hinted that the government was considering a legal tool that would protect the largest trees in the province from logging. New optimism bloomed in 2017, when a coalition of New Democratic Party and Green Party was elected to replace Christy Clark and the Liberals, to much celebration from West Coast environmentalists. While the new government quickly stated it could not commit to a full moratorium on old-growth logging, it announced "a new policy is being developed to protect iconic trees in B.C." On January 1, 2018, B.C. Timber Sales, the agency that has managed the timber harvested off public land on behalf of the provincial government since 2003, released a best-practices guideline for retaining "legacy trees" — those exceptionally large trees on the coast that "are increasingly supporting the growing ecotourism economy as valuable destinations in and of themselves." The guideline noted minimum diameters for various species including western red cedar, Sitka spruce, and Douglas fir that would place them off limits to logging, but noted that "it is up to the judgement of the assessor to use both estimated measurements and quality indicators to determine if a tree qualifies as a legacy tree suitable for retention."

It was a step forward, but one that gave little assurance to activists concerned about placing the onus of protection into the hands of a logger. Just months after the guideline was released, the ninth largest Douglas fir in British Columbia was felled along with its old-growth grove in the Nahmint Valley on Vancouver Island. In the wake of public outcry, the B.C. government announced that it will review its policy.

As governments delay, timber companies continue to cut ten thousand hectares of old-growth forests on Vancouver Island every year — three square metres every second. But Ken Wu can't help but look to one tree as a symbol of hope, the one tree at the centre of this legislative push: "This will be the legacy of Big Lonely Doug."

It will also be the legacy of the logger who saved one tree, but in the end might protect many. The way forward through the seemingly impenetrable forest may not be sparked by a protester chaining herself to a logging truck, but from the simple act of a logger saving a single tree — and doing more for the protection of old-growth forests than any march or barricade.

A YEAR AFTER HER husband died, Lorraine Cronin made the short drive from her home in Lake Cowichan to visit Big Lonely Doug. It was a cloudy day, overcast and dreary as so many spring days are on the West Coast. But the low cloud and pillows of mist softened the edges and brought the world in close. The last time she had stood under the tree was with Dennis, in his final year.

Lorraine took a detour first, up the steep switchbacks to near the top of a mountain where the head of Port San Juan and a few buildings of Port Renfrew came into view in the distance below. She parked her truck along the side of the logging road by a recent clear-cut. The clouds threatened a downpour but held back. The path to the wreckage of the Avro Anson plane found by her husband and his crew was marked along the scattered clear-cut with small holes in the logs from the spikes of timber workers' caulk boots—some undoubtedly left by Dennis. She moved slowly over the logs, careful not to slip, until she found the forest trail marked by a piece of ribbon dangling from a tree.

The first sign of anything unnatural within the forest was flakes of yellow paint, some the size of a fingernail, others as large as a hand. After more than seventy years, the Second World War aircraft appeared to have been well consumed by the undergrowth. But with each step closer to the crash site, bent pieces of metal stuck out among the salal and sword fern. A large cedar broken halfway up its trunk marked the beginning of the wreckage—Dennis Cronin had wondered if the plane had struck the tree when it ploughed through the forest.

Then, among the trees: an engine with a bent propeller, parts of the wooden fuselage still intact after three-quarters of a century, an electronic board with circuits and wires, and an unbroken lightbulb. A mound of metal fragments lay collected to one side from when the military team and archaeologists had combed the wreckage, looking for remains or personal effects. Lorraine beamed with pride at the thought that her husband had helped solve the mystery of the missing plane, and helped descendants in Britain find closure.

The mist on the mountain grew thicker as Lorraine returned to her truck and began the cautious drive down the steep logging road. She drove past a line of cars parked at the trailhead to Avatar Grove, where hikers and tourists were taking pictures under Canada's Gnarliest Tree. She kept going without pause. After fifteen minutes, she took the first right off the Gordon River Main Line logging road and crossed the bridge high over the churning water.

"My kids used to call this Daddy's Bridge," she said, explaining how Dennis had been part of the crew that had it initially installed.

She continued on as the road steepened to a grade only manageable by a four-wheel-drive vehicle, past the plantations of second-growth forest, and past the overlook built by Teal Jones road builders to haul the logs out of cutblock 7190.

Two vehicles were parked alongside the dirt road near the trail leading down to Big Lonely Doug. The first belonged to the crew of photographer Edward Burtynsky, whose team was operating a drone to capture images of the tree. The second vehicle, a blue Mitsubishi Delica van, belonged to TJ Watt, the Ancient Forest Alliance activist and photographer who had helped launch the tree into the limelight.

Lorraine sighed. She was hoping for a quiet moment. She parked her truck, put on her jacket, and started down the trail to the tree. Squatting on a stump halfway down was Watt, who was providing an overview perspective to help the drone operator.

"My husband saved that tree," Lorraine said, her voice quivering yet direct. The activists claiming the "discovery" of the tree always made her feel like what Dennis had done was being overshadowed.

"We're thankful for it," Watt replied.

For years, Watt had wanted to sit down with Lorraine Cronin to have a conversation about how their work isn't meant to be combative or aggressive towards timber workers and their families. On that misty day, the two forces that made Big Lonely Doug—the widow of the logger who flagged it and the activist who promoted it—had collided by happenstance under the great tree's boughs.

Lorraine looked across the cutblock to Big Lonely Doug, turned, and headed back up the trail to her truck. Halfway down the path was as close as she could get to the tree her husband had saved. It was a start.

The whirl of the drone kicked up, its helicopter-like blades buzzing as the man with the controller navigated it up and down and around the trunk of the enormous tree. The photographs were to be stitched together to form the high-definition, 360-degree image for their augmented reality exhibition.

Lorraine shut the door to her truck. The fog had condensed to a light drizzle and tears began welling in her eyes. It was an odd moment for her. Big Lonely Doug is more than just a big tree her husband saved. It has become a monument of sorts—a twenty-storey-tall tombstone to a man who loved the forests.

That same month, the South Island Natural Resource District designated Big Lonely Doug a recreational reserve as per the Forest and Range Practices Act. From there, the "minister may order the establishment of Crown land as an interpretive forest site, a recreation site or a recreation trail." It is a designation that has been given to other significant trees in the area, including the Red Creek Fir and the Harris Creek Spruce, which stand outside formal protection areas such as a provincial park. If turned into a recreational site, it would be promoted and advertised formally by the provincial government, luring a new wave of tourists to keep the lonely tree company. The recreation officer gave the reserve the forest file identification number REC230530—not quite as emotive as the name bestowed by the activists. Despite expressing caution about the bridge leading to the tree, Teal Jones was not void of support for turning the tree into a destination—only the timber company's representatives preferred not to use the name "Big Lonely Doug" but "Dennis Cronin Memorial Tree" instead.

It took a millennium for this Douglas fir to turn from one of a million seedlings sprouting along the Gordon River near Port Renfrew into one of the largest trees in Canada. But within the few short years since Dennis Cronin paused under the tree and tied a piece of green ribbon around its base, the tree has grown exponentially in renown. It became Big Lonely Doug—a tourist site and a rallying point for environmental activists; a symbol of the future of logging and the future of Vancouver Island's ancient forests. It went from a tree surrounded by forest to a tree in a wasteland to a tree known around the world.

Sitting in the cab of her truck, Lorraine Cronin stared with watery eyes at the Douglas fir in the middle of a clear-cut, watching the branches softly tremble in the breeze. She thought of her husband, Dennis, and shook her head ever so slightly.

"It's just a tree."

Notes

CHAPTER 2: EVERGREEN

Meidinger, Del, and Jim Pojar, eds. *Ecosystems of British Columbia*. Victoria: B.C. Ministry of Forests, February 1991.

Sierra Club of Western Canada and the Wilderness Society. *Ancient Rainforests at Risk: An interim report by the Vancouver Island Mapping Project*. Victoria: 1991.

Allen, George S., and John N. Owens. *The Life History of Douglas-fir*. Ottawa: Environment Canada, Canadian Forestry Service, 1972. https://doi.org/10.2307/1296578.

"On definitions of forest and forest change." Food and Agriculture of the United Nations, November 2, 2000. http://www.fao.org/docrep/006/ad665e/ad665e00.htm.

Global Forest Resources Assessment 2010. Rome: Food and Agriculture Organization of the United Nations, November 2, 2010.

Venkateswarlu, D. "Definition of forests: A review." New Delhi: Teri University. http://www.teriuniversity.ac.in/mct/pdf/assignment/VENKATESWARLU.pdf.

Sexton, Joseph O., Praveen Noojipady, Xiao-Peng Song, Min Feng, Dan-Xia Song, Do-Hyung Kim, Anupam Anand, Chengquan Huang, Saurabh Channan, Stuart L. Pimm, and John R. Townshend. "Conservation policy and the measurement of forests." *Nature Climate Change*, October 5, 2015. https://doi.org/10.1038/nclimate2816.

Centre for Forest Conservation Genetics, University of British Columbia. ClimateBC/WNA/NA program. doi: http://cfcg.forestry.ubc.ca/projects/climate-data/climatebcwna/.

Jones, Charles. *Queesto: Pacheenaht Chief by Birthright.* British Columbia: Theytus Books, 1981.

Arima, E.Y. *The West Coast People: The Nootka of Vancouver Island and Cape Flattery.* Victoria: British Columbia Provincial Museum, 1983.

Finkbeiner, Ann. "The Great Quake and the Great Drowning." *Hakai Magazine*, September 14, 2015. https://www.hakaimagazine.com/features/great-quake-and-great-drowning/.

Tindall, D. B., Ronald L. Trosper, and Pamela Perreault, eds. *Aboriginal Peoples and Forest Lands in Canada.* Vancouver: UBC Press, 2013.

Archaeology Branch, B.C. Ministry of Small Business, Tourism and Culture. *Culturally Modified Trees of British Columbia: A handbook for the identification and recording of culturally modified trees.* British Columbia: Resources Inventory Committee, March 2001. https://www.for.gov.bc.ca/hfd/pubs/docs/mr/mr091/cmthandbook.pdf.

"Man must apologize for cutting old trees." *Canadian Press*, November 16, 2001.

Banner, Allen, and Philip LePage. "Long-term recovery of vegetation communities after harvesting in the coastal temperate rainforests of northern British

Columbia." *Canadian Journal of Forest Research* 38, no. 12 (2008): 3098–3111. https://doi.org/10.1139/X08-145.

Moldenke, Andrew. "Small in Size, Great in Importance: Invertebrates in your soil." *Northwest Woodlands Magazine* (Summer 2001).

Silva Ecosystem Consultants. *Old Growth Literature Review.* May 1992.

Menary, David. *Great Trees of Canada.* Indianapolis: Blue River Press, 1997.

Nelson, John David. *A Vanishing Heritage: The Loss of Ancient Red Cedar from Canada's Rainforests.* Vancouver: Western Canada Wilderness Committee, 2004.

Morales-Hidalgo, David, Sonya N. Oswalt, and E. Somanathan. "Status and trends in global primary forest, protected areas, and areas designated for conservation biodiversity from the Global Forest Resources Assessment 2015." *Forest Ecology and Management* 352 (September 2015): 68–77. https://doi.org/10.1016/j.foreco.2015.06.011.

CHAPTER 3: TREE OF MANY NAMES

Lindsay, Ann, and Syd House. *The Tree Collector: The Life and Explorations of David Douglas*. London: Aurum Press, 2005.

Hooker, W. J. "Companion to the Botanical Magazine." Vol. II, 1896.

"Four of Britain's tallest trees in glen near Inverness." BBC News, March 25, 2014.

Douglas, David. *Journal Kept by David Douglas during his Travels in North America: 1823–1827*. New York: Cambridge University Press, 2011.

Harvey, Athelstan George. *Douglas of the Fir: A Biography of David Douglas, Botanist*. Cambridge: Harvard University Press, 2014.

Nisbet, Jack. *The Collector: David Douglas and the Natural History of the Northwest*. Seattle: Sasquatch Books, 2010.

Newcombe, C. F., ed. *Menzies' Journal of Vancouver's Voyage: April to October, 1792*. Victoria: William H. Cullin, 1923.

"The discovery of gold in California," *The Century Magazine* 4 (November 1880 to April 1891).

Murchison, Roderick Impey. "Siberia and California." *The Quarterly Review* 87 (1850): 395–434.

Shakespeare, Mary, and Rodney H. Pain. *West Coast Logging 1840–1910*. National Museum of Man, Mercury Series. Ottawa: National Museums of Canada, 1977.

Davidson, John. *Conifers, Junipers and Yew: Gymnosperms of British Columbia*. London: T. F. Unwin, 1927.

Lauriault, Jean. *Identification Guide to the Trees of Canada*. Markham: Fitzhenry and Whiteside, 1989.

Hansen, Carl. "Pinetum Danicum." *Journal of the Royal Horticultural Society of London*, vol. XIV (1892).

Parminter, John. "A Tale of a Tree." *British Columbia Forest History Newsletter*, no. 45 (January 1996).

Gould, Ed. *Logging: British Columbia's Logging History*. Blaine, WA: Big Country Books, 1975.

Robson, Peter A., Art Walker, and the Working Forest Project. *The Working Forest of British Columbia*. British Columbia: Harbour Publishing, 1995.

Sculland, Keri. "Old forests get protection." *Alberni Valley Times*, August 5, 2010.

Sauder, E. A., and G. V. Wellburn. *Planning Logging: Two Case Studies on the Queen Charlotte Islands, B.C.* Vancouver: Forest Engineering Research Institute of Canada, September 1989. https://www.for.gov.bc.ca/hfd/pubs/docs/mr/Lmr/Lmr059.pdf.

Foster, R. E., G. P. Thomas, and J. E. Browne. "A Tree Decadence Classification for Mature Coniferous Stands." *The Forestry Chronicle* 29, no. 4 (1953): 359–366.

Silva Ecosytems Consultants. *Old Growth Literature Review*. May 1992.

CHAPTER 4: GREEN GOLD

Rajala, Richard. *The Legacy and the Challenge: A Century of the Forest Industry at Cowichan Lake*. Lake Cowichan: Lake Cowichan Heritage Advisory Committee, 1993.

Gould, Ed. *Logging: British Columbia's Logging History.* Blaine, WA: Big Country Books, 1975.

Hayman, John, ed. *Robert Brown and the Vancouver Island Exploring Expedition.* Vancouver: UBC Press, 1989.

Jones, H. H. "A cyclone among the Timber Titans," *British Columbia Magazine,* vol. VII (1911).

"British Columbia's Forest Policy: Speech by the Hon. William R. Ross, Minister of Lands, on the second reading of the Forest Bill." Legislative session of 1912.

Saywell, John F. T. *Kaatza: The Chronicles of Cowichan Lake.* Sidney: Cowichan Lake District Centennial Committee, 1967.

Gillis, R. Peter, and Thomas R. Roach. *Lost Initiatives: Canada's Forest Industries, Forest Policy and Forest Conservation.* New York: Greenwood Press, 1986.

Drushka, Ken. *Canada's Forests: A History.* Montreal: McGill-Queen's University Press, 2003.

Rajala, Richard Allan. *Clearcutting the Pacific Rain Forest: Production, Science, and Regulation.* Vancouver: UBC Press, 1998.

Province of British Columbia. *Report of the Forest Branch of the Department of Lands 1913*. https://www.for.gov.bc.ca/hfd/pubs/docs/mr/annual/ar_1911-30/annual_1913.pdf.

Andrews, Ralph W. *This Was Logging: Drama in the Northwest Timber Country*. Atglen, PA: Schiffer Publishing, 1997.

Mackie, Richard. *Mountain Timber: The Comox Logging Company in the Vancouver Island Mountains*. Winlaw, B.C.: Sono Nis Press, 2009.

Pearce, Peter H. "Evolution of the forest tenure system in British Columbia." Vancouver: February 1992.

Turner, Robert D. *Logging by Rail: The British Columbia Story*. Winlaw, B.C.: Sono Nis Press, 1990.

Wolfe, Linnie Marsh. *John of the Mountains: The Unpublished Journals of John Muir*. Madison: University of Wisconsin Press, 1979.

Köhl, Michael, Prem R. Neupane, and Neda Lotfiomran. "The impact of tree age on biomass growth and carbon accumulation capacity: A retrospective analysis using tree ring data of three tropical tree species grown in natural forests of Suriname." *PLoS ONE* 12, no. 8 (August 16, 2017). https://doi.org/10.1371/journal.pone.0181187.

Oregon State University. "Oldest trees are growing faster, storing more carbon as they age." *ScienceDaily*, January 15, 2014. https://www.sciencedaily.com/releases/2014/01/140115132740.htm.

S. J. and Jessie E., Quinney College of Natural Resources, Utah State University. "Inequality is normal: Dominance of the big trees." *ScienceDaily*, May 8, 2018. https://www.sciencedaily.com/releases/2018/05/180508155029.htm.

Stephenson, N. L., et al. "Rate of tree carbon accumulation increases continuously with tree size." *Nature* 507 (March 6, 2014): 90–93. https://doi.org/10.1038/nature12914.

Faculty of Forestry, University of British Columbia. "The Pacific Salmon Ecology and Conservation lab." *Branchlines* 27, no. 1 (Spring 2016).

Adams, Megan S., Christina N. Service, Andrew Bateman, Mathieu Bourbonnais, Kyle A. Artelle, Trisalyn Nelson, Paul C. Paquet, Taal Levi, and Chris T. Darimont. "Intrapopulation diversity in isotopic niche over landscapes: Spatial patterns inform conservation of bear–salmon systems." *Ecosphere* 8, no. 6 (June 2017). https://doi.org/10.1002/ecs2.1843.

Babikova, Zdenka, Lucy Gilbert, Toby J. A. Bruce, Michael Birkett, John C. Caulfield, Christine Woodcock, John A. Pickett, and David Johnson. "Underground signals carried through common mycelial networks warn neighbouring plants of aphid attack." *Ecology Letters* 16, no. 7 (July 2013): 835–843. https://doi.org/10.1111/ele.12115.

Beiler, Kevin J., Daniel M. Durall, Suzanne W. Simard, Sheri A. Maxwell, and Annette M. Kretzer. "Architecture of the wood-wide web: Rhizopogon spp. Genets link multiple Douglas-fir cohorts." *New Phytologist* 185, no. 2 (January 2010): 543–53. https://doi.org/10.1111/j.1469-8137.2009.03069.x.

Simard, Suzanne W., Kevin J. Beiler, Marcus A. Bingham, Julie R. Deslippe, Leanne J. Philip, and François P. Teste. "Mycorrhizal networks: Mechanisms, ecology and modelling." *Fungal Biology Reviews* 26 (2012): 39–60. https://doi.org/10.1016/j.fbr.2012.01.001.

Twieg, Brendan D., Daniel M. Durall, and Suzanne W. Simard. "Ectomycorrhizal fungal succession in mixed temperate forests." *New Phytologist* 176, no. 2 (October 2007): 437–47.

Simard, Suzanne W. "Unseen Connections." In *We Discover*, edited by Marc Guttman. 2016. www.wediscover.net.

Sierra Club B.C. "Twenty-five international environmental organizations call for urgent action for Vancouver Island's rainforest and communities." April 10, 2017. https://sierraclub.bc.ca/25-international-environmental-organizations-call-for-urgent-action-for-vancouver-islands-rainforest-and-communities/.

Sierra Club B.C. "Sierra Club B.C.'s Google Earth tool shows Vancouver Island old-growth in a state of emergency." March 30, 2016. https://sierraclub.bc.ca/sierra-club-bcs-google-earth-tool-shows-vancouver-island-old-growth-state-emergency/.

CHAPTER 5: WAR FOR THE WOODS

Sloan, Gordon McG. *Report of the Commissioner, the Honourable Gordon McG. Sloan, Chief Justice of British Columbia, relating to the Forest Resources of British Columbia, 1956*. Victoria: Don McDiarmid, 1957. https://www.for.gov.bc.ca/hfd/pubs/docs/mr/rc/rc004/Rc004-1.pdf.

Utzig, G. F., and D. L. Macdonald. *Citizens' Guide to Allowable Annual Cut Determinations: How to Make a Difference.* Vancouver: British Columbia Environmental Network Education Foundation, 2000.

Hume, Mark. "Tree team tracking giant spruce." *Vancouver Sun*, May 14, 1988.

Western Canada Wilderness Committee. *Carmanah Forever* (film). 1988. https://www.wildernesscommittee.org/video/1988_04_15_carmanah_forever.

George, Paul. *Big Trees Not Big Stumps: 25 Years of Campaigning to Save Wilderness with the Wilderness Committee.* Vancouver: Western Canada Wilderness Committee, 2006.

Hume, Mark. "Carmanah road building halted." *Vancouver Sun*, May 19, 1988.

Hume, Mark. "Record spruce elusive, but big ones abound." *Vancouver Sun*, May 17, 1988.

Hume, Mark. "Woodsman spare that tree." *Vancouver Sun*, June 11, 1988.

"Most of the valley productive forest," *The Province*, April 11, 1990.

"Save the Carmanah and save the murrelets," *Vancouver Sun*, December 2, 1989.

Stanbury, William T. *Environmental Groups and the International Conflict over the Forests of British Columbia, 1990 to 2000*. Vancouver: SFU-UBC Centre for the Study of Government and Business, 2000.

Salazar, Debra J., and Donald K. Alper, eds. *Sustaining the Forests of the Pacific Coast: Forging Truces in the War in the Woods*. Vancouver: UBC Press, 2000.

Western Canada Wilderness Committee. *Visions of Carmanah* (film). 1989.

Carr, Emily. *Hundreds and Thousands: The Journals of Emily Carr*. Vancouver: Douglas & McIntyre, 1966.

Western Canada Wilderness Committee. *Suzuki Kids in Carmanah Valley* (film). 1990. https://www.wildernesscommittee.org/video/1990_05_23_suzuki_kids_carmanah_valley.

MacMillan Bloedel. *The Incredible Forest* (film). Canadian Forest Industries Films. Montreal: 1976.

MacMillan Bloedel. *The Managed Forest* (film). 1986.

Rowell, Andrew. *Green Backlash: Global Subversion of the Environment Movement*. New York: Routledge, 1996.

Niosi, Goody. *Magnificently Unrepentant: The Story of Merve Wilkinson and Wildwood*. Surrey, B.C.: Heritage House Publishing, 2001.

Meikle, Graham. *Future Active: Media Activism and the Internet*. New York: Routledge, 2002.

Wilson, Jeremy. *Talk and Log: Wilderness Politics in British Columbia*. Vancouver: UBC Press, 1998.

Bohn, Glenn. "Arrests, injury, and tree spiking escalate battle over Walbran." *Vancouver Sun*, September 24, 1991.

Bohn, Glenn. "Environmentalists spiked for bounty." *Vancouver Sun*, April 24, 1991.

Boei, William. "Clayoquot Sound: 200 litres of human excrement dumped at anti-logging group's information tent." *Vancouver Sun*, August 4, 1993.

Forest Resources Commission. *The Future of Our Forests: Executive Summary.* Victoria: B.C. Ministry of Forests, 1991.

CHAPTER 6: A FOREST ALLIANCE

Ancient Forest Alliance. "New B.C. organization 'Ancient Forest Alliance' launched to protect B.C.'s old-growth forests and forestry jobs." January 19, 2010. https://www.ancientforestalliance.org/news-item.php?ID=1.

Ancient Forest Alliance. "An exceptionally spectacular and accessible stand of newly located old growth red-cedars and Douglas firs near Port Renfrew has recently been marked for logging." February 18, 2010. https://www.ancientforestalliance.org/news-item.php?ID=10.

Ancient Forest Alliance. "Earth Day media release: Avatar's James Cameron invited by environmental group to visit the endangered 'Avatar Grove' of ancient trees." April 22, 2010. https://www.ancientforestalliance.org/news-item.php?ID=55.

"James Cameron: Fox didn't want Avatar's 'treehugging crap,'" *USA Today*, February 19, 2010. http://content.

usatoday.com/communities/greenhouse/post/2010/02/james-cameron-fox-didnt-want-avatars-treehugging-crap/1#.WvsjZjKZP-Y.

George, Paul. *Big Trees Not Big Stumps: 25 Years of Campaigning to Save Wilderness with the Wilderness Committee.* Vancouver: Western Canada Wilderness Committee, 2006.

Ancient Forest Alliance. "The 'gnarliest tree in Canada' found in the endangered 'Avatar Grove' on Vancouver Island in British Columbia." March 25, 2010. https://www.ancientforestalliance.org/news-item.php?ID=33.

Lavoie, Judith. "B.C. chops down bid to protect 'Avatar Grove.'" *Vancouver Sun*, August 5, 2010.

Forest Practices Board. *Logging Old-Growth Forest Near Port Renfrew.* Victoria: February 2011.

Ancient Forest Alliance. "Breaking News: Avatar Grove might get saved—please write a letter now!!" February 12, 2011. https://www.ancientforestalliance.org/news-item.php?ID=196.

Lavoie, Judith. "Island version of Avatar Grove given provincial protection." *Times Colonist*, February 17, 2012.

Gardner, Sheila. "Forest alliance welcomes government announcement to preserve Avatar Grove." CFAX, February 16, 2012.

"Protection of Avatar Grove will boost tourism." *Sooke News Mirror*, February 22, 2012. https://issuu.com/sooke-mirror/docs/snmn_2012_02_22.

"British Columbia: clearcutting the 'Avatar Forest.'" *Pacific Free Press*, February 19, 2010.

Ancient Forest Alliance. "Stunning grove of unprotected old-growth trees located near Port Renfrew." May 11, 2017. https://www.ancientforestalliance.org/news-item.php?ID=1120.

Ancient Forest Alliance. "Magnificent Old-Growth Forest found on Vancouver Island—11 foot wide, near-record size Sitka spruce towers in 'FernGully Grove.'" December 15, 2017. https://www.ancientforestalliance.org/news-item.php?ID=1156.

Ancient Forest Alliance. "Christy Clark Grove." April 20, 2012. https://www.ancientforestalliance.org/news-item.php?ID=413.

"Ancient grove named for premier." *Sooke News Mirror*, April 25, 2012. https://www.sookenewsmirror.com/news/ancient-grove-named-for-premier/.

Klem, Greg. "Avafraud Grove." *Sooke News Mirror*, April 13, 2011. https://www.sookenewsmirror.com/opinion/avafraud-grove/.

Wu, Ken. "Avatar Grove must get saved." *Sooke News Mirror*, April 12, 2011. https://www.sookenewsmirror.com/opinion/avatar-grove-must-get-saved/.

CHAPTER 9: GROWING AN ICON

Ancient Forest Alliance. "Canada's most significant big tree discovery in decades!" March 21, 2014. https://www.ancientforestalliance.org/news-item.php?ID=753.

Hume, Mark. "Canada's loneliest tree still waiting on help." *Globe and Mail*, June 9, 2014. https://www.theglobeandmail.com/news/british-columbia/canadas-loneliest-tree-around-1000-years-old-still-waiting-on-help/article19064507/.

Stoltmann, Randy. *Hiking Guide to the Big Trees of Southwestern British Columbia.* Vancouver: Western Canada Wilderness Committee, 1987.

Jones, H. H. "A Cyclone among Timber Titans." *British Columbia Magazine*, vol. VII (1911).

CHAPTER 10: BIG TREE HUNTING

The University of British Columbia. B.C. BigTree Registry. http://bigtrees.forestry.ubc.ca.

CHAPTER 11: TALL TREE CAPITAL

Goldman, Josephine. *Pioneer Days of Port Renfrew.* Privately printed, 1973.

Norcross, E. Blanche, and Doris Farmer Tonkin. *Frontier Days of Vancouver Island.* Courtenay, B.C.: Island Books, 1969.

Lunman, Kim. "Life at sawmill faces final cut." *Globe and Mail*, January 20, 2001. https://www.theglobeandmail.com/news/national/life-at-sawmill-faces-final-cut/article1029767/.

Parfitt, Ben. *Getting More from Our Forests: Ten Proposals for Building Stability in B.C.'s Forestry Communities*. Vancouver: Canadian Centre for Policy Alternatives, December 2005.

Ancient Forest Alliance. "Horgan, Hicks, and Cash join Ancient Forest Alliance on tour of Avatar Grove and to Canada's biggest trees and stumps." September 28, 2010. https://www.ancientforestalliance.org/news-item.php?ID=136.

Britten, Liam. "BC Hydro buys out properties below Jordan River dam." CBC News, May 17, 2016. http://www.cbc.ca/news/canada/british-columbia/b-c-hydro-jordan-river-1.3585351.

CHAPTER 12: A NEW ECOSYSTEM

Leiren-Young, Mark. *The Killer Whale Who Changed the World*. Vancouver: Greystone Books, 2016.

"Berlin zoo: Brain problems led to death of polar bear Knut." *Toronto Star*, March 22, 2011. https://www.thestar.com/news/world/2011/03/22/berlin_zoo_brain_problems_led_to_death_of_polar_bear_knut.html.

B.C. Ministry of Forests and B.C. Ministry of Environment. *Forest Practices Code of British Columbia: Biodiversity Guidebook*. Victoria: 1995. https://www.for.gov.bc.ca/hfd/library/documents/bib19715.pdf.

British Columbia Forest Service. "The Retention System: maintaining forest ecosystem diversity." *Notes to the Field* 7 (March 2002). https://www.for.gov.bc.ca/hfp/publications/00095/note_07.pdf.

Stoltmann, Randy. *Hiking Guide to the Big Trees of Southwestern British Columbia*. Vancouver: Western Canada Wilderness Committee, 1987.

Lavoie, Judith. "Retired logger ready to renew fight to save fir; magnificent old-growth stand viewed as being under threat despite logging company's denials." *Times Colonist*, May 23, 2007.

Bainas, Lexi. "Old-growth grove faces saws yet again." *Cowichan News Citizen*, May 25, 2007.

"Old-growth trees not coming down." *Cowichan News Citizen*, May 30, 2007.

Wilson, Carla. "Fallers persuade logging bosses to spare centuries-old fir grove." *Times Colonist*, May 4, 1989.

"Climbing Mount Everest is work for superman." *New York Times*, March 18, 1923.

EPILOGUE: A GIANT

B.C. Timber Sales. "Best Management Practices for Coastal Legacy Trees." https://www.for.gov.bc.ca/ftp/tsg/external/!publish/EMS2/Supplements/TSG-BMP-CoastalLegacyTrees.pdf.

Pynn, Larry. "Call to protect B.C.'s 100 top heritage trees." *Vancouver Sun*, January 31, 2009.

Acknowledgements

I am so grateful for all the timber workers, environmental activists, members of the Pacheedaht First Nation, residents of Port Renfrew, ecologists, and experts in their various fields who took the time to speak or take a walk in the woods with me, with special mention to Dennis and Lorraine Cronin, TJ Watt, Jeff Jones, Mark Carter, Ken Wu, Walter Van Hell, Dan Hagar, Greg Klem, Kristine Pearson, Bear Charlie, Arnie Bercov, Torrance Coste, Andy MacKinnon, Hans Tammemagi, Joe and Karen Simpson, Matthew Beatty, and Ray Travers, among many others.

I am thrilled that *Big Lonely Doug* is the inaugural title in the Walrus Books imprint at House of Anansi Press. Thanks to Shelley Ambrose, executive director and publisher of *The Walrus*, and Sarah MacLachlan, president and publisher of Anansi, for their enthusiasm for this story. Research and reporting for this book simply would not have been possible without support from the Chawkers Foundation Writers Project, for which I am deeply grateful.

A special thanks to Carmine Starnino, deputy editor at *The Walrus* magazine, for editing my original article that appeared in the October 2016 issue, and for helping me hone the story into one about us—our relationships, our motivations, our emotions—as much as one about a tree. I'm so proud the article resonated with so many people, won a silver National Magazine Award, and was reprinted in *Reader's Digest Canada*—and I owe a great deal to him for championing the story.

I am exceptionally grateful to Janie Yoon, my editor at House of Anansi, for her vision when it came to expanding this story and for her sharp yet kind editing. I could not have asked to be in better hands for my first book. And to everyone at Anansi—including managing editor Maria Golikova, for patiently fielding all my extremely basic questions about how a book is made, Alysia Shewchuk for the beautiful cover design, Gemma Wain for her detailed copyediting and vital fact-checking, and Peter Norman for the final proofread.

I have been extremely fortunate to have learned from and worked under some generous and talented journalists and writers early in my career. I would like to thank University of King's College professor David Swick for his mentorship and friendship; Stephanie Nolen for accepting my plea to intern for her at the *Globe and Mail*'s South Asia bureau in New Delhi, India; and Matthew McKinnon, editor and former colleague at *The Walrus*, for his guidance and encouragement in writing and editing. And thanks to author Kevin Patterson for lending me his sailboat, where I managed an important breakthrough in the writing of this book despite never untying from the dock, and for being so relentlessly positive.

Writing this book was often an isolating experience. I was so grateful for a group of friends in Toronto who met in the University of King's College's journalism program—Geoff Lowe, Julia Pagel, Thea Fitz-James, Miles Kenyon, Laura Bain, Kevin Philipupillai, and Laura Armstrong—who have all made that big city with its tiny trees feel like home.

To my sisters, Britta and Clare, for adventuring in the forests together, looking for "watermelon slices," when we were young, and to my mum and dad for constantly surrounding me with books and magazines and newspapers and stories—and for never telling me to climb down from that tree.

Index

activists vs. loggers
arrests of activists, 92, 104, 112, 219
Avatar Grove value, 133
Carmanah Valley, 91–100, 105, 112–113
Clayoquot Sound, 112–113
loggers' cynicism, 105, 113, 179, 190–191
meaning of trees, 88
media campaigns, 105–108
saving Big Lonely Doug, 238
See also direct action; environmental activists; loggers
Adams, Bryan, 104
adopt-a-tree campaign, 101, 206
alder trees, 28, 169
allowable annual cut (AAC), 86
Ancient Forest Alliance (AFA)
AFA platforms, 121–122
Big Lonely Doug recreational reserve application, 209–211
broader mobilization, 121–123, 128–130, 134–135, 205, 213, 219–220, 259
campaigns with Big Lonely Doug, 177–179, 200–201, 206, 213
community meetings, 219–220
Eden Grove, 145–146, 257–259
speculating about Big Lonely Doug, 235–236
tourism, 142–145
See also Avatar Grove; Watt, TJ; Wu, Ken
Anderson sawmill, 54
Anthropocene (film), 265
Arboreal Collective, 199
artists, 102–105
augmented reality installations, 266–267
Avatar (film), 128–129
Avatar Grove
AFA finding, 127–129

cynicism regarding, 147–148, 179, 228–229
the Gnarly Tree, 133–134
managing, 230
naming of, 129, 130
Pacheedaht people and, 131–132, 228–229
protection of, 139–140, 210
Teal Jones and, 141–142
as tourist destination, 132–133, 135–136
Avro Anson L7056 airplane, 244–245, 272–273

Bateman, Robert, 102
B.C. BigTree Registry, 194–196, 194–197
B.C. Forest Alliance, 108
B.C. Timber Sales, 270
bears, 78–79, 260–261
Beatty, Matthew, 199
Bell, Pat, 136, 138, 139, 140–141, 269–270
Bens, Samuel J., 65
Bercov, Arnie, 118, 262–265
Big Lonely Doug
in 3D, 3–4, 274–275
age of, 204–205
as anchor, 178–179
Burtynsky and, 266–267
as captivating, 160, 205–206, 251–252
climbing, 198–202
Cronin finding, 9–11, 159–161
as endangered, 180–181, 182–185, 188, 247
height of, 202–203
leaving intact, 235–236, 238, 242, 243
location and visitors, 207
logging responsible for, 246
marking, 11
as monument, 275
as recreational reserve, 209–211, 275–276
root networks, 248
status and, 197
sun catching, 165
as symbol, 175–176, 178–179, 207–208, 235, 267–268
in tampon commercial, 208
Watt finding, 170, 172–173
Wu first view, 174–175
Big Tree Protection Order, 269
biodiversity, 52
See also biomass
Biodiversity Guidebook, 237–238
biogeoclimatic zones, 16–17
biomass, 23
botanizing missions, 34–39
bristlecone pine trees, 203–204
British Columbia, 16–17, 71–72
See also Vancouver Island
British Columbia Lumber Company, 214
Brown, Robert, 56
burls, 134
Burson-Marsteller company, 108
Burtynsky, Edward, 264–267

California Gold Rush, 55–56
Cameron, James, 129
candelabra tops, 127
Carmanah: Artistic Visions of an Ancient Rainforest, 105
Carmanah Forever (film), 99–100
Carmanah Giant, 88–89, 93–96, 100–101, 111

Carmanah Valley, 88–94, 96–105
Carmanah Walbran Provincial Park, 111, 113, 144
Carr, Emily, 102–103, 171
Carter, Mark, 141
Cary, George, 45
Cary fir, 45
cedars, 3, 20, 29, 127, 133–134, 159–160
chainsaws, 65–66
chambers of commerce, 222–224
Charlie, Bear, 226, 228
Clark, Christy, 145
Clayoquot Sound, 104, 112, 236
clear-cutting
  artists' views of, 104–105, 171
  early concern, 59–61
  inventory on Vancouver Island, 82–84
  marking trees, 5–9, 11
  monitoring, 24
  roads, 8–9
  root networks and, 81
  second-growth forests, 52–53, 74–75, 81, 103, 248–250
  timber companies' views of, 106
  visual descriptions, 51, 53, 104–105, 167, 171
  See also activists vs. loggers; cutblock 7190; cutblocks; environmental activists; loggers; logging industry; old-growth forests; timber companies
Coastal Douglas Fir zone, 17
Coastal Western Hemlock zone, 17
Coast Salish people, 18–19
colonization, 35
  See also botanizing missions; settlers
Columbia River, 32, 35
cones, 1–2, 41–42
conservation
  B.C. BigTree Registry, 197
  early, 59–61, 62–63
  and economics, 230
  as emotional, 101–102, 200, 205
  for root networks, 81–82
  See also environmental activists
Cook, James, 31–32
Council of Forest Industries, 106
Cronin, Dennis
  activists and, 188–191
  captivated by Big Lonely Doug, 160, 251–252
  cutblock 7190 trees, 183–184
  death of, 254
  Eden Grove and, 258
  finding Avro Anson L7056, 244–245
  finding Big Lonely Doug, 9–11
  finding CMTs, 243–244
  guessing age of Big Lonely Doug, 205
  illness, 253–254
  as logger, 5–11, 152–161
  protecting Big Lonely Doug, 160–161, 238–239, 242, 243
  Steller jay and, 153–154
Cronin, Lorraine, 158–159, 191, 251–252, 271–272, 274–275, 276
culturally modified trees (CMTs), 20–22, 131, 226, 243–244

See also Indigenous Peoples
cutblock 7190, 6–11, 153–155, 183–184, 247–250, 253
See also Big Lonely Doug
cutblocks, 51–53, 81, 166, 238
See also clear-cutting; loggers; logging industry
"A Cyclone Among the Timber Titans" (Jones), 185–186

Deakin, Alfred, 214
"Dennis Cronin Memorial Tree"
See Big Lonely Doug
Diitiida River/Jordan River, 19, 21
direct action
against activists, 112
blockades Clayoquot Sound, 104
blockades of Queen Charlotte Islands, 92
confusing loggers, 190–191
dismissed, 213
vs. education, 120–121
GDP and, 219
Pacheedaht support and, 146
tree sitting, 109, 200
tree spiking, 109–110, 190
See also activists vs. loggers
donkey engine, 67–68
Dorst, Adrian, 100–101
Douglas, David
collecting samples, 34, 36–37, 38–39, 55, 56
on the Columbia River, 32, 35–36
death of, 40
description of Douglas fir, 37–38
as Horticultural Society explorer, 33–35, 39–40, 42–43
interest in Douglas fir, 37, 56
taxonomic name Douglas fir, 41, 43
value of wood, 46–47
vernacular name Douglas fir, 43
Douglas fir
description of, 29–30, 37–38, 42, 44
diameter of, 27
falling, 181–182
heartiness of, 47–48, 159–160
height of, 17, 27, 40–41, 44–46, 179–180
lifespan, 3, 10
locations of, 44
logging industry and, 48–49, 57
and marbled murrelets, 26
oldest in 1957, 239–240
photograph controversy, 45–46
Red Creek Fir, 10
as roads, 48
root networks, 80, 81
in shipbuilding, 47
taxonomic names of, 41–43
See also Big Lonely Doug

economics, 60–63, 87, 93–95, 135–136, 213, 221–223, 230
Eden Grove, 145–146, 257–259, 268
Edinburgh Mountain, 150–151, 163, 165, 168–169, 172, 211
See also Big Lonely Doug
Elm Conflict, 200

environmental activists
broader mobilization, 199–201, 259 (*see also* Ancient Forest Alliance)
Carmanah Valley importance, 92
Clayoquot Sound, 104
climate change, 120
definitions of old-growth, 24–25
as "eco-terrorists," 108–109
focus on positives, 124
Indigenous Peoples and, 131, 142–143, 146
photography as effective, 175
rise of, 87–88
as salespeople, 179
Sierra Club B.C. and Vancouver Island, 83
subvertisements, 106–107
symbols needed, 175
tree-centric concerns, 209
tree sitting, 109
tree spiking, 109–110
unions and, 262–263
variable retention and, 236
See also activists vs. loggers; Ancient Forest Alliance; Avatar Grove; direct action; Stoltmann, Randy; Watt, TJ; Western Canada Wilderness Committee; Wu, Ken
Expo 67, 48

fallers
See loggers
FernGully Grove, 145
fire, 22–23, 47–48, 61–62
Fletcher Challenge, 240–241
fog, 14–15
Forest Act, 59–60, 116
forest buffers, 180–181, 182–185, 188, 201, 269
forest engineers, 7–8, 157
See also Cronin, Dennis
forest management, 85–87, 106–107
Forest Practices Board (FPB), 137–138, 140
Forest Practices Code of British Columbia Act / Forest and Range Practices Act, 113, 115–116
forestry code, 7
forests
death in, 72–73
definitions, 24–25
as spiritual, 123
Forest Service, 61, 62, 91
"Forests Forever" campaign, 107
Fortune, Robert, 34–35
Foy, Joe, 110
fungi, 6, 26, 76–77, 79–81, 248
The Future of Our Forests (Forest Resources Commission), 113

George, Paul, 88, 92, 95–96, 99, 120
Gnarly Tree, 133–134
gold rush, 54–57
Gordon River, 6–7
Gordon River Valley, 126, 136, 145, 166
See also Avatar Grove; Big Lonely Doug
Great Bear Rainforest, 115
Greenpeace, 112

greenwashing, 107
Gye, Mike, 89

Hagar, Dan, 218–219, 220–221, 224
Haida people, 92
Halpert, George, 20
Heaven Tree, 93
hemlock trees, 28, 73
high riggers, 68–69
Hiking Guide to the Big Trees of Southwestern British Columbia (Stoltmann), 90, 130
Hill, Julia "Butterfly," 200
historic logging
  early concern, 59–63
  early falling methods, 64
  Indigenous Peoples, 18–22, 131, 226, 243–244
  settlers, 32, 53–54, 58–64
  See also loggers; logging industry
Hooker, William Jackson, 37
Horticultural Society of London, 33–34, 36, 39, 42–43, 55–56
Hudson's Bay Company, 32, 54
Hughes, Don, 240–241
Hundreds and Thousands (Carr), 103
Hyperion, 45

The Incredible Forest (film), 106
Indigenous Peoples
  as activists, 92
  activists and, 131, 142–143, 146
  Avatar film and, 129
  botanists and, 35
  culturally modified trees (CMTs), 20–22, 131, 226, 243–244
  as early loggers, 18–20, 193
  passing big trees, 197
  settlers and, 29
  stumpage fees, 227, 263
  West Coast Trail, 216
  See also Nuu'chah'nulth people; Pacheedaht people
Interfor, 115–116

Jakubal, Mikal, 200
Jones, H. H., 58, 185–186
Jones, Jeff, 143, 226, 227–228, 229–230
Jordan River (town), 217–218
Journal of the Royal Horticultural Society (journal), 42–43
Jurassic Grove, 144

kayaking, 223
Kinsol Trestle, 71
Kitsumkalum First Nation, 20
Klem, Greg, 148–150
Knut (polar bear), 234–235
Koksilah Grove, 239–241
Kroitor, Christian, 264
Kwakwaka'wakw people, 18–19

Lake Cowichan, 156, 254
Lasn, Kalle, 106–107
legacy trees, 270–271
lightness / darkness, 27–28
loggers
  antipathy towards activists, 105, 112–113, 179, 190–191
  in British Columbia, 66–69
  chainsaws, 65–66
  chokermen jobs, 67, 69

early tree cutting, 64
(*see also* historic logging)
faller jobs, 66–69, 162
feller bunchers, 64–65
Forest Act and, 59–61
high rigger jobs, 68–69
hooktender jobs, 67, 162
job losses, 96–97, 118–119
jobs in British Columbia, 71–72
media usage, 105–107
as protectors, 270–271
refusing to cut, 240–241
sentiment on old-growth, 74
in storm, 185–187
transportation, 162
tree spiking and, 109–110, 190
unions, 262–265
work-related deaths, 67, 69–70, 109
See also activists vs. loggers; clear-cutting; Cronin, Dennis; timber companies; Van Hell, Walter
logging industry
best-practices guide, 270
conglomerates, 217
deception, 119
deregulation, 115–117
evolving communities, 155–156
expansion, 63–64
expansion and Douglas fir, 48–49
expectations of, 263–265
historic logging, 131, 214, 226, 243–244
impatience, 249–250
local processing, 118–119
logging as obligation, 61–63, 73–74, 74
loopholes for clear-cutting, 139
mandatory replanting, 87
selective logging, 236–237
transportation, 57–58, 63–64, 67–71, 214–215
trusting, 242
variable retention, 236
(*see also* clear-cutting)
Lord of the Rings (Tolkien), 130
Lumpy tree, 149

MacKinnon, Andy, 184–185, 187–188
MacMillan, Harvey Reginald (H. R.), 62
MacMillan Bloedel
Carmanah Giant and, 89, 93–95, 97, 99
Carmanah Valley logging, 91–95, 111
marketing films, 106
oldest Douglas fir and, 240
on tree spiking, 109
See also Weyerhaeuser
Mallory, George, 242
The Managed Forest (film), 106
Manufactured Landscapes (film), 265
maple trees, 28
marbled murrelets, 26
McClure, John, 185–186
McMullan, Don, 240
measuring trees, 10, 61, 93, 202–203, 204
Menzies, Archibald, 39, 41, 56
Methuselah tree, 203–204

Moby Doll orca, 234
Muir, John, 47, 72, 83
mycorrhiza, 76–77, 79–81, 248

new ecosystem, 233–234
Nitinat Valley, 57
Nootka Sound, 32, 39
nurse logs, 73
Nuu'chah'nulth people, 18–19, 31

o.b. company, 208
old-growth forests
  age of, 23–24, 137–138
  animals in, 6–7, 26, 78–79
  composition of, 22, 24–25, 37–38, 75
  culturally modified trees and, 22
    (*see also* culturally modified trees)
  death in, 72–73
  definitions, 18, 23–25
  as disordered, 257–258
  dwindling, 5, 258
    (*see also* clear-cutting)
  as ecological emergency, 83
  inventory on Vancouver Island, 82–84, 258, 270
  legacy trees, 270–271
  locations of, 22
  logging industry sentiment and, 74
  pictures evoked, 17
  vs. second-growth forests, 52, 81
  as soil filter, 7
  sounds in, 6
  underground structure, 75–77, 79–81
  See also rainforests (temperate)
old-growth management area (OGMA), 139–141

Pacheedaht people
  activists and, 131–132, 142–143, 146
  benefits of Tall Tree Capital, 225–226
  controlling territory, 229–230
  as guides, 228–229
  as loggers, 19, 21–22
  protecting Big Lonely Doug, 210
  sawmill, 226–227, 229–230
  Teal Jones and, 229
Pacific Ocean, 13–14, 15, 78, 182, 216
Pacific temperate rainforests
  See rainforests (temperate)
Patagonia company, 207–208
Pearson, Kristine, 132, 230
Pegg, Mike, 180
photography
  See Burtynsky, Edward; Watt, TJ
Port Alberni, 61
Port Renfrew, 177, 196, 213–222, 224–225
  See also Avatar Grove; Big Lonely Doug; cutblock 7190
Port San Juan, 19
Prometheus tree, 204
Public and Private Workers of Canada, 262–263

Queen Charlotte goshawk, 26

rain, 15, 17, 216
rainforests (temperate)
  animals in, 26, 261
  artists' views of, 104
  Big Lonely Doug and, 268
  biomass, 23
  canopy of, 101, 126
  as cathedrals, 27–28
  colours in, 126–127
  composition of, 17–18
  historic logging, 18, 19–21, 32
  locations of, 15–16
  tree cutting processes, 65–69
  tree growth, 75, 77, 79–80, 88
  valleys of, 14–15, 88
  See also old-growth forests
raw logs, 117–119
Red Creek Fir, 174
replanting, 87
Richardson, Kelly, 264
root networks, 76–77, 79–81
Ross, William Roderick, 59–60

salmon, 6–7, 19, 78–79
sawmills, 53–54, 96, 115–117, 226
Scorned as Timber, Beloved of the Sky (Carr), 104
second-growth forests, 52–53, 74–75, 81, 103, 248–250
seedlings, 2–3
seeds, 1–2
  See also cones
sequoia trees, 45
settlers, 29–32, 47
Shadbolt, Jack, 102
Shawnigan Lake, 70–71
Sierra Club, 83
Simard, Suzanne, 76–77, 80–81
Simpson, Joe, 251–252
Simpson, Karen, 251–252
Sitka clothing company, 207
Sitka spruce
  Carmanah Giant, 89, 90, 93–94
  Cronin and, 157
  description of, 29
  Douglas and, 36
  FernGully Grove, 144–145
  Heaven Tree, 93
  height of, 3
  Van Hell Spruce, 239
Sloan, Gordon, 85–87
Sloan Commission, 85–87
social media, 125
Sombrio Beach, 216–217
Species at Risk Act, 26
Stamp, Edward, 54
Steep Trails (Muir), 47
Steller jay, 153–154
Stoltmann, Randy, 88, 89–91, 93, 96, 145, 194–195
storms/wind, 13, 15, 134, 181–185, 186–187, 188, 255
stumpage fees, 119, 227, 263
Stumpy (tree stump), 112
sun, 15
Suzuki, David, 99–100, 147

Tall Tree Capital
  See Port Renfrew
Tammemagi, Hans, 136–137
taxonomy, 41–43
Teal Jones
  Big Lonely Doug bridge and, 210–211
  compensation to, 140–141

culturally modified trees
and, 226
logging practices, 137, 138,
258–259
marking trees, 128
Pacheedaht people and, 229
processing logs, 117–118
protecting Big Lonely Doug,
161–162, 235–236
See also Cronin, Dennis
threatened species, 26
thujaplicin, 73
timber companies
definitions of old-growth,
23–25
media campaigns, 105–107,
108
pressure within, 96–97
stumpage fees, 61
See also clear-cutting; Forest
Act; Forest Service; logging
industry; MacMillan Bloedel; Teal Jones; TimberWest;
Weyerhaeuser
timber industry
See logging industry
timber licences (TLs), 58
TimberWest, 115–116, 117
timber workers
See loggers
Tofino, 219
tree climbing, 199–202
tree farm licences (TFLs), 86, 91,
99, 111, 141
tree hugging, 205
tree hunting, 88–91, 93–94,
150–151, 167–169, 193–194,
197–198, 251
See also tree registry
tree registry, 194–197
See also tree hunting
trees (general)
coastline trees, 13–14
wildlife tree, 237–238
tree sitting, 109, 200
tree spiking, 109, 190
trucks, 71

unions, 262–265

Van Beers, Louie, 240–241
Vancouver Island
coastline of, 13–16
fires in, 22–23
inventory of old-growth,
270
as model, 263
old-growth decline, 258
Vancouver Island Ranges,
15–16
Van Hell, Walter, 154, 158,
161–162, 239, 258
Van Hell Spruce, 239
Victoria, B.C., 48

Waddington Alley, 48
Walbran Valley, 110, 111,
125–126, 228
War in the Woods, 104, 112, 236
Watermark (film), 265
Watt, TJ
about, 124–125
climbing Big Lonely Doug,
197–199, 202
discovery and, 257–258
dispirited about Big Lonely
Doug, 172–173
in Eden Grove, 257–260, 268

enthusiasm for Big Lonely Doug, 173–175, 176
on FernGully Grove, 145
finding Avatar Grove, 128
finding Big Lonely Doug, 166–170
finding the Gnarly Tree, 133–134
meeting Lorraine, 274–275
photographing Big Lonely Doug, 175–176
as tree hunter, 125–126, 127–128, 133–135, 166–170
TV interviews, 189
urging governments, 178
See also Ancient Forest Alliance (AFA)
Webb, Clinton, 90–91, 194
Welter, T. W., 185
West Coast Trail, 216
Western Canada Wilderness Committee (WCWC)
about, 88, 92
B.C. BigTree Registry, 194–196
B.C. legislature protest, 129–130
broader mobilization, 129–130
Carmanah Giant protests, 92–95, 97–101, 104–105, 110
as charity, 122
War in the Woods, 112
Wu and George, 120–121
See also Stoltmann, Randy
Western Lumberman (magazine), 45–46
western red cedars, 3, 20, 133–134, 159–160
Weyerhaeuser, 115–116
See also MacMillan Bloedel
Whistler, 220
wildlife tree, 237–238
wind/storms, 13, 15, 134, 181–185, 186–187, 188, 255
Wu, Ken
about, 120–121
B.C. legislature protest, 129–130
on Big Lonely Doug legacy, 271
Big Tree Protection Order, 269
dismissing hypocrisy, 143
on destruction, 262
Eden Grove and, 145–146
as filmmaker, 261–262
first view of Big Lonely Doug, 174–175
on logging industry practices, 178
meeting with Bell, 139
on Pacheedaht sawmill, 226–227
promoting Avatar Grove, 128–129, 130, 133, 142
starting AFA, 121–124
Tofino and, 219
TV interviews, 189
urging governments, 181
See also Ancient Forest Alliance; Avatar Grove

Author photograph: Harley Rustad

HARLEY RUSTAD is an editor at *The Walrus* magazine. His articles and photography have been published in *The Walrus*, *Outside*, the *Globe and Mail*, *Geographical*, CNN, and elsewhere. He has reported from India, Nepal, Cuba, and across Canada. Born on Salt Spring Island, B.C., he lives in Toronto.

@hmrustad
harleyrustad.com